Christmas Doughcrafts

Christmas Doughcrafts

LORRAINE BODGER

Illustrated by Lorraine Bodger

Sedgewood® Press
New York

AUTHOR'S ACKNOWLEDGMENTS

I could not have completed this book
without the fine products supplied by my
colleagues at the American Tree Company
and the Wrights Home Sewing Company,
on whom I have come to depend. Wrights
provided the beautiful ribbons, cords
and trims used for making the ornaments
and other projects, and American Tree
loaned me the handsome trees and wreaths
used in the photography. Many thanks
to both.

FOR SEDGEWOOD® PRESS

Director: Elizabeth P. Rice
Associate Editor: Leslie Gilbert
Project Editor: Miriam Meyer
Production Manager: Bill Rose
Designer: Betty Binns Graphics
Photographer: Robert Epstein
Photo Stylist: Lorraine Bodger

Distributed by Macmillan Publishing Company, a division of Macmillan, Inc.

ISBN   0-02-496770-X

Library of Congress Catalog Card Number 85-63722

Printed in the United States of America

First printing 1986

10 9 8 7 6 5 4 3 2 1

Contents

Chapter 3 The Twelve Days of Christmas Tree

Chapter 4 Wreaths

Chapter 5   Setting a Christmas Table: Centerpieces, Table Decorations and Cookie Creations

Chapter 6   Wall Decorations

This is the second book I have written about doughcrafts. If you have read the first book, *Woman's Day Doughcrafts*, then some of the material in Chapter 1 is familiar to you—basic information about flour/salt dough, bread/glue dough and other things. Even so, please read this chapter to find new techniques, hints and recipes. You will probably want to brush up on your basics anyway.

If you're a newcomer to doughcrafts, all of Chapter 1 is unexplored territory, so read it carefully. It tells you everything you need to know about making the different doughs, how to work with them and what equipment you need. Refer to this chapter whenever you start a doughcrafts project. You will see that none of the information is difficult to understand, all of the materials are easily acquired—and your imagination will be off and running.

Of course, all the projects in *Christmas Doughcrafts* are brand-new, designed especially for this book. I think you'll find plenty of inspiration for making your home a Christmas delight.

USING THE BOOK: CHRISTMAS AROUND YOUR HOUSE

There are two specific ways to use this book: one, reproduce any of the projects exactly as they are shown in the photographs; two, adapt any project to suit your particular situation. For example, if you like the Christmas Stocking Wreath on page 99 but you've already made a decorated wreath, make the stocking ornaments anyway—and hang them on your Christmas tree instead. Or perhaps you like the little mosaic tiles you see on the Framed Christmas Pictures (page 156) but you haven't got a spare inch of wall space. Make the tiles anyway—and use them to decorate a few special Christmas cards. Almost any project in the book can be altered or adapted to a special need, so feel free to do so.

INVENTING YOUR OWN ORNAMENTS

In addition to making the projects in this book, you will eventually want to make ornaments and other Christmas doughcraft items of your own design. Here's a way to get your toes wet: Simply start off with a basic design of mine and change the decorations and colors to match your style. For example, let's take those stockings from the Christmas Stocking Wreath (page 99) again. You've got the basic pattern for the stocking; now try some trims and colors of your own.

From this simple approach you'll find you can go on to more ambitious original designs.

GENERAL TECHNIQUES FOR WORKING WITH DOUGH

There are five doughs used in this book: flour/salt dough; bread/glue dough; cornstarch dough; cookie dough; and gingerbread dough. Although they are made of different ingredients, there are several techniques applicable to working with all five doughs. Read these general techniques before you go on to read about working with each specific dough.

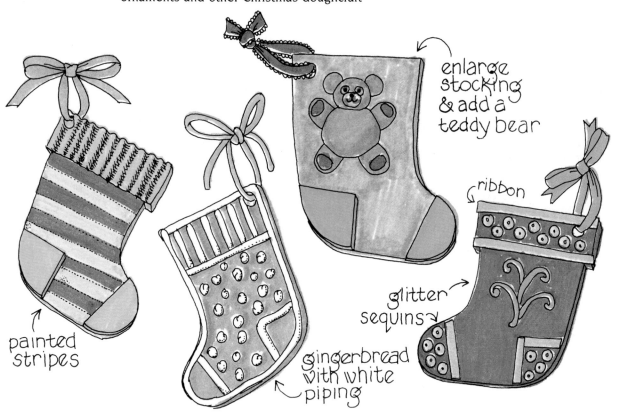

enlarge stocking & add a teddy bear

ribbon

glitter sequins

painted stripes

gingerbread with white piping

1. Rolling out the dough

The trick for rolling out an even layer of dough is to use a good, heavy rolling pin and two strips of wood as supports for the rolling pin.

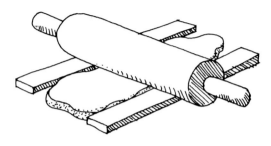

Usually the dough must be rolled out to ¼″ thick or ⅛″ thick, so have on hand one pair of strips ¼″ thick and another pair ⅛″ thick. I use balsa-wood strips, but you might prefer basswood or even pine lattice.

Dust the work surface with flour (or cornstarch, if you are working with cornstarch dough). Pat the dough into a rectangle and place it on the work surface. Put a strip of wood on each side of the dough and begin rolling out the dough firmly. Keep rolling until the rolling pin comes to rest on the wood strips.

2. Rolling the dough into a rope

Dust the work surface with flour (or cornstarch, if you are working with cornstarch dough). Break off a small piece of dough and roll it back and forth to make a long, even rope.

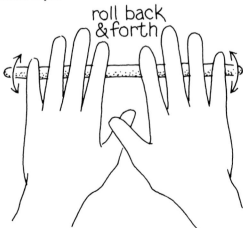

roll back & forth

3. Rolling bits of dough into balls or ovals

Break off small pieces of dough and roll each one between your palms to make a solid, round ball. A round ball can then be rolled to an oval shape.

4. Cutting the rolled dough with cookie cutters, canapé cutters and/or aspic cutters

Many of you already have wonderful collections of cookie cutters—scalloped rounds, hearts, animals, Christmas trees and angels. Depending on which projects you choose to do, a set of canapé cutters and a set of aspic cutters will come in handy, too. My favorite canapé cutters come in two sizes and four shapes; my best set of aspic cutters has a tiny heart, diamond, star, teardrop, crescent and several other shapes.

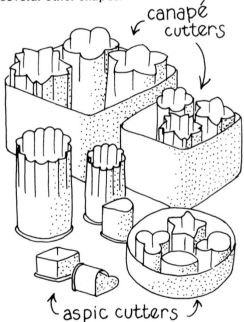

canapé cutters

aspic cutters

Dust your work surface with flour (or cornstarch) and roll out some dough according to general technique #1 (page 11). Dip a cookie (canapé, aspic) cutter in flour (or cornstarch) and press it firmly into the dough. Repeat to cut as many cookies or dough shapes as needed. Gather up the excess dough, knead it together and rewrap it tightly in plastic.

5. Molding the dough by hand

Simply break off a piece of dough and shape it by hand, following the instructions in the project. Most of the hand-molded shapes required in this book are quite simple; as you become more accomplished in working with dough, you may want to attempt more intricate molded shapes.

6. Cutting the rolled dough freehand, with a sharp knife

If you need some simple shape, e.g., a diamond, it is often easier just to pick up a sharp knife and cut the rolled dough, rather than try to find the correct size of cookie cutter or make a special pattern for cutting the diamond. For best results, use a knife with a smooth (not serrated) blade and wipe the blade often to keep it clean. Cut slowly and firmly without dragging the blade through the dough. Long, straight cuts can also be made with a long spatula.

7. Cutting the rolled dough with a template and a sharp knife

The instructions for some projects include full-size patterns which must be transferred from the book page to thin cardboard to make templates. A template is used for making multiples of an ornament or project: Place a template on rolled-out dough, hold it lightly in position and carefully cut around it with a sharp knife. Lift away the excess dough and the template, and you have a dough copy of the pattern in the book. Use the template over and over again to make as many ornaments as you need.

NOTE: If the dough is sticky, dust it with flour (or cornstarch, if you are working with cornstarch dough) before placing the template on it, so the template doesn't stick to the dough.

Here's how to make the template:

■ Place a piece of tracing paper over a pattern in the book. With pencil or pen, copy the pattern onto the tracing paper.

■ Put a sheet of ordinary carbon paper, ink side down, on a piece of thin cardboard (shirt cardboard, oaktag, poster board, etc.). Place the tracing paper on top of the carbon paper and draw firmly over the outline with pencil or ball-point pen.

Remove the tracing and carbon papers and cut the cardboard on the outline. This cutout is the template.

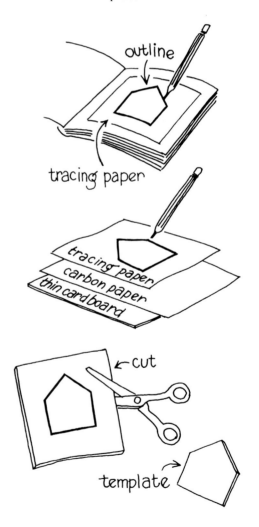

outline

tracing paper

tracing paper
carbon paper
thin cardboard

cut

template

8. Putting a hole or a paper clip loop in an ornament

Most of the ornaments in the book require a hole or a wire loop through which to thread a piece of ribbon or cord. The ribbon or cord is then tied to the Christmas tree or to a wreath. (See page 14, *Hanging the doughcraft ornaments.*)

■ Use a plastic drinking straw to make a hole in the ornament: Press the end of the straw firmly through the dough and withdraw it. A disk of dough will be withdrawn with the straw.

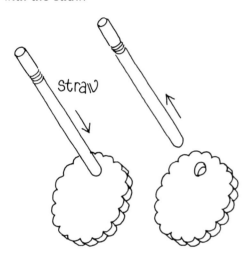

■ Use a narrow plastic straw to make a hole in the ornament: This kind of straw is often used for stirring and sipping a cocktail. Press the end firmly through the dough and withdraw it, removing a disk of dough.

■ Use the blunt end of a wooden skewer to make a hole in the ornament: Press the blunt end into the dough and move it gently in a circular direction to enlarge the hole to the size specified in the instructions. Be sure the hole is clean and goes all the way through the dough. Turn the ornament over if possible and repeat from the back.

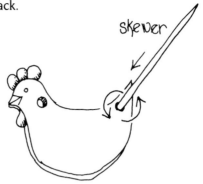

■ Make a paper clip loop for the ornament: You will need some regular-size steel paper clips (shown actual size in the drawing) and a wire cutter. Bend the clip open and cut with the wire cutter, as shown, to make two U-shaped loops. Depending on the size of the ornament, use the smaller or larger loop and cut down the shanks if necessary. Insert the ends of the loop into the top of the ornament, centering them in the thickness of the dough. Be sure to push the ends far enough into the dough; there should be only about $1/4''$-$3/8''$ of paper clip showing above the edge of the ornament.

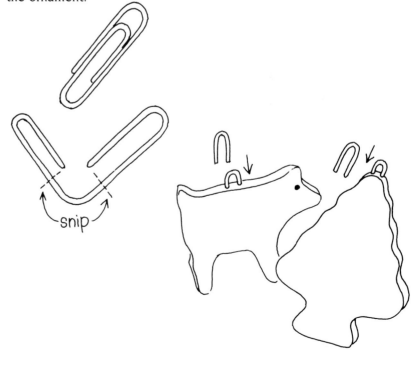

HANGING THE DOUGHCRAFT ORNAMENTS

Most of the ornaments are hung on the Christmas tree or wreath with pieces of ribbon. Some are attached with yarn, soutache, rickrack or standard ornament hooks. There are a variety of techniques, as you will see in the photographs and drawings; each individual project tells you which method to use. Here is a rundown of these methods:

1. Fold a piece of ribbon in half and push the ribbon loop up through the hole in the ornament or through the paper clip loop. Slip the ends of the ribbon through the ribbon loop and pull them tight. Tie the ends to the tree.

2. Fold a piece of ribbon in half and glue the ends to the back of the ornament. Slide the ribbon loop over a tree branch.

3. Glue two pieces of ribbon to the back of an ornament. Tie the free ends over a tree branch.

4. Fold a piece of ribbon in half and push the ends up through the hole in the ornament. Tie the ends in a pretty bow on the front and then slide the ribbon loop over a tree branch.

5. Slip one end of the ribbon through the hole in the ornament. Tie the ends of the ribbon in a knot and slide the ribbon loop over a tree branch OR tie the ends in a bow over a tree branch.

6. Slip one end of the ribbon through the ornament itself and tie the ends in a bow over a tree branch.

7. Fasten a wire ornament hook to the paper clip loop in an ornament. Slip the hook over a tree branch.

8. Push one end of the ribbon through one hole in the ornament; tie the ribbon to itself, making a double knot above the ornament. Push the other end of the ribbon through the second hole in the ornament and adjust the length of the ribbon. Tie the ribbon to itself, making another double knot above the ornament. Trim off the excess ribbon.

9. Tie a knot near one end of the ribbon. Thread the unknotted end up through one hole and back down through the second hole, adjusting the length of the ribbon. Make a knot in the second end. Trim off the excess ribbon. **NOTE:** The knots are on the *front* of the ornament.

WORKING WITH ADHESIVES

There are only three adhesives used in this book—Sobo glue, 527 cement and five-minute epoxy. If an adhesive is needed for a project, it is listed in the *Materials* column for that project.

SOBO GLUE: Sobo is a white, liquid glue, similar to other white glues but better in quality and longer lasting. It comes in a squeezable plastic container with a pointed tip. Look for it in art supply, craft supply and hardware stores; if you can't locate Sobo in your area, use the best white glue you can find.

There are several ways to work with Sobo. You can apply it directly to the ornament (or whatever you are working on) from the container; you can pour a small amount out onto a piece of waxed paper and use your finger, a toothpick or a paint brush to apply the glue to the ornament; you can pour a little glue onto waxed paper and use tweezers to pick up a small item (for example, a petal, leaf or bead), dip it in glue and then place the item in position on the ornament.

527 CEMENT: 527 is a high-quality clear cement that comes in a metal tube with a pointed metal tip. Buy it in craft supply and hardware stores; if you can't get it in

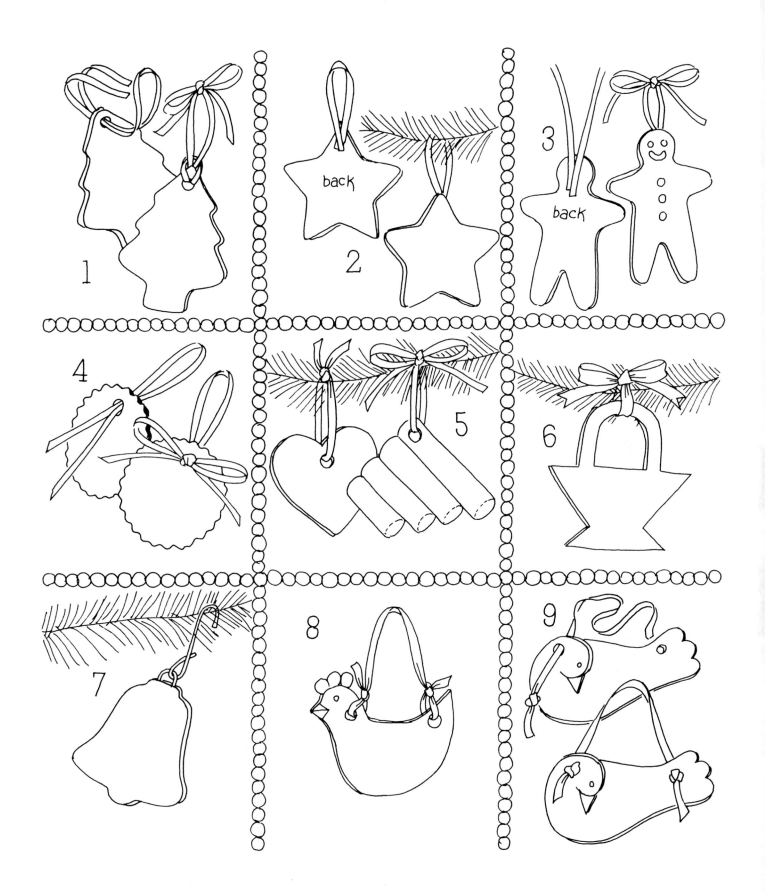

your area, get the best clear cement you can find.

You must use 527 straight from the tube, since it will dry too quickly if you pour it out onto waxed paper.

FIVE-MINUTE EPOXY: Epoxy is a very strong glue made of two thick liquids (each in its own container) that must be mixed together. Epoxy is available at the five-and-ten and in hardware stores.

Squeeze equal amounts of each liquid onto a piece of cardboard or waxed paper and mix them thoroughly with a toothpick. Mix only as much as you need at one time, since the epoxy dries so rapidly. Use the toothpick to apply the epoxy where it is needed. Let it dry overnight to get the full benefit of the bond.

Flour/salt dough

INGREDIENTS

4 cups all-purpose flour

1 cup salt (iodized or plain)

1½ cups water

If you look through the book, you will see that the majority of projects are made of flour/salt dough. This is an easy-to-make, easy-to-use dough of great versatility. You can roll it, cut it, mold it, braid it, even weave it. It is baked hard and then left as is (a pale tan), glazed to a shade of warm brown or painted in bright colors. The final step is to seal it with coats of polyurethane—and it should last for quite a long time.

In a big bowl, mix the flour and salt until blended. Add one cup of water and continue to mix. Slowly add the remaining half cup of water, turning the dough in the bowl. Push the dough into a ball, working in any flour and salt left at the bottom of the bowl. Knead the dough firmly for ten minutes, setting your kitchen timer to remind you. Wrap the dough tightly in plastic or put it in a plastic bag secured with a twist tie.

DOS AND DON'TS

Do cut the ball of dough in half and knead each piece separately for ten minutes if your arms are not very strong.

Do keep all pieces of dough not in use wrapped tightly in plastic.

Do store leftover dough in the refrigerator and use it within one week.

Do bring the refrigerated dough to room temperature before working with it.

Don't eat the dough!

PROBLEM-SOLVING:
TOO DRY OR TOO MOIST

When the dough is too dry, the edges split and crack and it won't hold together in a solid ball. Simply wet your hands and knead the dough some more, working the moisture from your hands into the dough. Repeat until the dough is malleable and smooth. Don't overdo it.

When the dough is too moist, it will lose shape and ooze through your fingers when you hold it in your hand. This weepy condition can be corrected by kneading the dough with a little more flour *and* salt. Mix ¼ cup flour with ¼ cup salt and use this mixture to dust your work surface. Knead the weepy dough on this surface, working in the flour and salt as you knead. Repeat until the dough is firm and smooth. Don't overdo this remedy either.

BASIC EQUIPMENT

The list below tells what equipment you will need for working with flour/salt dough; these items are not generally listed in the *Materials* column because I assume you have them handy.

- Tracing paper, carbon paper and thin cardboard for making templates
- Rolling pin
- 2 strips of wood, each ⅛″ thick; 2 strips of wood, each ¼″ thick. (See page 11, Technique #1.)
- Heavy-duty cookie sheets or jelly roll pans

NOTE: Projects can be baked on the *back* of a jelly roll pan; this is a good substitute if you don't have a second cookie sheet.

- Wire racks (the kind used for cooling cakes and cookies)
- Small spatula; long spatula
- Sharp knife
- Ruler
- Wooden skewers (ordinarily used for canapés and kebobs; buy them at gourmet and import stores)
- Round wooden toothpicks
- Plastic drinking straws and narrow plastic straws for making holes
- Small brush for applying water to dough
- Waxed paper

Anything else needed for a specific project will be listed in the *Materials* column—acrylic paints, polyurethane, brushes, glue, ribbon and so on.

WORKING WITH FLOUR/SALT DOUGH

Once the dough is made, you can start working with it immediately. Gather the basic equipment together, along with any special items listed in the *Materials* column. Dust your work surface with flour and follow the instructions for the project you have chosen. **NOTE:** Before you begin, be sure to brush up on the general techniques for working with dough (pages 10–13).

BEFORE BAKING: ATTACHING THE PARTS

Look at the photographs in the book. You can see that almost every flour/salt dough project and ornament is composed of parts that are attached—layered, side by side, decorative bits stuck on, etc.

Water, applied with your finger or a brush, is the "glue" that holds the parts together; use just enough to make a firm bond.

NOTE: Water discolors the dough during baking, so if you are making an item that will remain natural-colored or glazed (not painted), be careful where you brush water when you are attaching two parts; excess water makes blotches on the finished product.

BEFORE BAKING: DECORATING THE FLOUR/SALT DOUGH

1. Crimping: Press the dough firmly with the tines of a fork, without going all the way through, just as you would crimp the edge of a little apple turnover.

2. Incising: The dough is quite receptive to all kinds of marking and poking. You can incise a pattern or a mark with the blunt and/or pointed ends of a wooden skewer, with the end of a straw, back of a knife blade, or just about anything else. Incising must be done firmly, without going all the way through the dough, and it must be done before the surface of the dough air-dries.

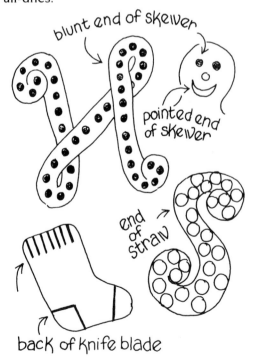

blunt end of skewer

pointed end of skewer

end of straw

back of knife blade

3. Adding shapes: Hearts, leaves, flowers, stars, ropes, berries and other dough shapes can be added to an unbaked dough ornament or project with just a bit of water acting as glue. Read the section called *Before baking: Attaching the parts* on page 18 for more information.

4. Adding garlic-press strands: The hair of the lord and lady ornaments (pages 90 and 83) is made by forcing a piece of dough through a garlic press. Force the dough through only until the strands are the length you want. Remove a group of strands by drawing a sharp knife along the garlic press at the base of the strands or remove a few strands at a time with a toothpick or wooden skewer. Brush water on the ornament and place the strands in position. Be sure to wash the garlic press carefully before leftover dough dries on it.

BEFORE BAKING: MAKING HOLES AND ADDING PAPER CLIP LOOPS

Many of the ornaments require either holes or paper clip loops through which you can thread ribbon or cord for tying the ornament to the Christmas tree. General instructions for making the holes and loops are given in Technique #8 on page 13.

BAKING THE FLOUR/SALT DOUGH

Every flour/salt dough project must be baked at low heat to a rocklike hardness; the instructions for each project tell you when to do this and how long to leave the item in the oven. In fact, the item is drying as much as it is baking, so baking times may range from half an hour for small items to several hours for large ones. The amount of time needed in the oven depends on the individual oven and the specific project.

Preheat the oven to 250°. Place the ornaments or project on a cookie sheet (or on the back of a jelly roll pan, according to the instructions) and put the sheet or pan in the oven. Some items must be baked without turning them over at all, others must be turned over on the cookie sheet and some are turned over onto a wire rack so the bottoms bake more easily; follow the instructions for that particular project. (**NOTE:** Place the wire rack on a cookie sheet, jelly roll pan or sheet cake pan so it can be removed conveniently.) At some point during the baking you will run a spatula under each item to loosen it from the cookie sheet; again, follow the individual instructions.

Each item must be baked until it is completely hard. The way to judge hardness is to remove the item from the oven, let it cool for a few minutes and then press it gently. If the dough gives, it is not baked enough. If it does not yield to the pressure of your finger, it is completely baked *on that side*. Turn the item over and repeat the test. If the underside is not firm, return the item to the oven and continue baking until it is completely hard.

PROBLEM-SOLVING: CRACKING, PUFFING AND WARPING DURING BAKING

It is characteristic of this kind of dough to puff up and warp a little during baking. It may even develop some small cracks. That much you can expect. However, sometimes, for no apparent reason, the dough goes berserk and *really* warps or even splits. There is no solution to this problem. It's a pity, but you must throw the piece out and start again.

AFTER BAKING: COOLING THE DOUGH

Let the baked items cool on the cookie sheet or on wire racks. Don't try to handle them or go on to the next step until they are completely cool. When they are cool, you may finish the items in one of three ways: with polyurethane; with paint and then polyurethane; with glaze and then polyurethane. Each project has specific instructions for finishing.

FINISHING WITH POLYURETHANE

All baked flour/salt dough projects, whether natural-color, painted or glazed, must be brushed with several coats of polyurethane. Polyurethane is a clear liquid sealer that comes in satin finish for a slight shine or gloss finish for a pronounced shine. Whichever you prefer, buy the highest quality you can afford. Apply it with an ordinary paint brush; it dries in a few hours or overnight to form a hard, protective coating.

Natural-color (unpainted and unglazed) projects may be brushed first with a half-and-half mixture of turpentine and polyurethane stirred together in a small jar. Brush the mixture on one side of the item and set aside to dry on waxed paper. When that side is dry, turn the item over and brush the mixture on the other side. Let that side dry thoroughly. Then brush on two, three or four coats of undiluted polyurethane, following the same general procedure: do one side, allow it to dry on waxed paper, turn it over and do the other side. You must allow each coat to dry completely before applying the next. The process may take several days.

Leave your brush in a small jar of turpentine between coats. When you have finished, clean the brush first in turpentine and then with cold water and ordinary hand soap. Be sure to remove all the polyurethane from the brush or it will stiffen up and be unusable.

FINISHING WITH PAINT AND POLYURETHANE

Most of the flour/salt dough projects in this book are painted with acrylic paints and then finished with a few coats of polyurethane. Acrylic paints are extremely easy to use, since they are thinned with water (the brushes are cleaned in water, too) but they are not water-soluble when they dry. And you certainly don't have to be an artist to do the simple kind of painting required in these projects.

Tubes of acrylic paint are available in any art supply store. You may, of course, buy just the colors needed for a specific project, but if you are going to do a few projects, it's a good idea to buy the basics: Titanium White; Cadmium Red Medium; Cadmium Yellow Medium; Ultramarine Blue; Cobalt Blue; Permanent Green Light; Permanent Green Dark; Burnt Sienna. Other colors you may need are Opaque Gold, Opaque Silver, Yellow Oxide, Acra Red and Burnt Umber.

At the same time you buy your paints, buy three good medium-priced brushes: one small, pointed brush; one larger, pointed brush; one wide, flat brush for covering large areas. Use these brushes only for painting; buy a less expensive brush for polyurethaning the work.

You will also need a pad of disposable palettes. These are pieces of waxed white paper on which you mix your paint; throw away the used paper when you finish painting for the day.

Now you are ready to begin painting. Before you paint *color* on any baked dough item, paint it white: Place the item on a piece of waxed paper and paint the front and sides white. Let the front dry thoroughly. Turn the piece over, paint the back white and let it dry thoroughly.

The instructions for each project tell you what colors to paint and the photographs give you guidance as well, but feel free to invent your own color scheme for any project. Most colors require two coats to achieve opacity, so when you are mixing up a color (as opposed to using the color straight from the tube), mix enough to cover the area twice. The paints are easy to work with, but they do dry quickly—an advantage when you are waiting to paint another coat or color but a disadvantage when you want to save some carefully mixed color. For this reason, many of the colors I used came straight from the tube.

The same general procedure applies to painting colors as to painting white: Paint the front and sides, let them dry and then paint the back. Let the back dry and repeat for a second coat.

When the paint is completely dry, brush the first coat of undiluted polyurethane on the front and sides of the item and let them dry. Turn over, brush polyurethane on the back and let the back dry. Repeat this procedure to apply two, three or four coats of polyurethane, letting each coat dry thoroughly before applying the next.

NOTE: If the item has holes for threading ribbon, be very careful not to clog them with paint or polyurethane.

FINISHING WITH GLAZE AND POLYURETHANE

Instead of baking a piece for long periods of time to achieve different shades of toasty brown, I have found that a simple glaze works just as well. Use this glaze when specified in the instructions. You must begin with a natural-color, unpainted, unsealed, unpolyurethaned piece, baked or unbaked.

INGREDIENTS

1 egg white

1 teaspoon water

1 teaspoon instant coffee

Stir the ingredients together in a little cup or jar; the color of the glaze may be lightened by adding a little more water or darkened by adding a little more instant coffee.

Paint the glaze lightly but thoroughly over the top and sides of the unbaked or baked and cooled item. If you are working on an unbaked piece, bake until hard; if you are working on a baked piece, bake only until the glaze is dry, about 10-15 minutes. You may repeat with another coat of glaze to get a darker color. The glaze may be stored in the refrigerator for several days only.

When the item is cool, apply several coats of undiluted polyurethane as explained in the previous section, *Finishing with paint and polyurethane*, page 20.

FINAL TOUCHES

Some of the finished projects require a bit more decoration. The decorations, attached with glue, might include other baked and finished dough pieces, trims (like rickrack and lace), sequins, glitter and crystal sugar. Follow the instructions for the specific project.

PROBLEM-SOLVING: REPAIRING CRACKS AND BREAKS

It is possible that your completely finished ornaments and projects will develop cracks and/or breaks. If an ornament or small piece breaks cleanly, glue the parts together with Sobo glue (see page 14): Apply glue evenly to one broken edge, press the two parts together, matching carefully, and hold them until the glue sets. Wipe away the excess glue with a damp paper towel or cotton swab. If a large item breaks, glue the pieces together with five-minute epoxy (see page 16), wiping away the excess glue with a lint-free rag.

Small cracks can be concealed by packing them with white acrylic paint and then repainting and polyurethaning over the repair. Larger cracks can be filled with ready-to-use spackle or caulking (be sure to wipe away any excess immediately) and then repainted and polyurethaned.

Bread/glue dough

INGREDIENTS

8 slices of day-old white bread (the less-expensive, fluffy kind)

½ cup Sobo glue

I always think of flour/salt dough as having a simple, expansive, rough-edged personality, while bread/glue dough is more precise and delicate. Bread/glue dough is very smooth, flexible and fine-grained, suitable for small-scale projects like ornaments or mosaic tiles. The dough itself is colored with paste food colors before you begin to work with it, not painted at a later stage, and it dries in the air, not in the oven. Although it can hold delicate shapes and impressions, it is quite sturdy when completely dry.

Cut the crusts—*only* the crusts—off the bread and discard them. Tear the bread into small pieces and put them into a bowl. Pour the glue over the pieces, stirring with a fork. Use one hand to mix the bread and glue into a sticky, well-blended ball. With both hands, pat the sticky dough into a neater ball and keep patting until the surface is just tacky. Dust flour on your work surface and begin to knead the dough gently. As it becomes smoother and more pliable, knead it firmly. Knead for about five minutes, until the dough is satiny. Wrap tightly in plastic or put in a plastic bag secured with a twist tie.

NOTE: If you need a larger amount of dough, use 12½ slices of bread and ¾ cup of glue.

DOS AND DON'TS

Do keep all pieces of dough not in use wrapped tightly in plastic.

Do store leftover dough in the refrigerator for up to several weeks.

Do bring the chilled dough to room temperature before working with it.

Don't eat the dough!

PROBLEM-SOLVING: TOO DRY OR TOO MOIST

This dough tends to dry out and stiffen if it is exposed to the air for any length of time, so knead a few drops of water into it now and then as you work. If you overdo the water and the dough gets sticky, knead in a little flour. As long as you correct the dryness or stickiness, the dough can be worked and reworked as much as you like.

BASIC EQUIPMENT

The list below tells what equipment you will need for working with bread/glue dough; these items are not generally listed in the *Materials* column because I assume you have them handy.

- Tracing paper, carbon paper and thin cardboard for making templates
- Rolling pin
- 2 strips of wood, each ⅛″ thick. (See page 11, Technique #1.)
- Waxed paper
- Wire racks (the kind used for cooling cakes and cookies)
- Scissors
- Small spatula; long spatula
- Ruler
- Wooden skewers (ordinarily used for canapés and kebobs; buy them at gourmet and import stores)
- Round wooden toothpicks
- Plastic drinking straws and narrow plastic straws for making holes
- Small brush for applying water to dough

Anything else needed for a specific project will be listed in the *Materials* column—garlic press, glue, glitter, ribbon and so on.

COLORING THE DOUGH

This dough should be tinted with food color before you begin to work with it. Ordinary liquid food color works adequately with bread/glue dough but it has two disadvantages: the extra liquid makes the dough sticky and the colored dough dries looking different from the way it looked when moist. For these reasons and to achieve generally brighter and prettier tones, I use paste food colors instead of liquid colors.

Buy the basic paste food colors (red, green, blue, yellow and brown) in little jars; they are inexpensive and last a long time since the color is extremely concentrated. In fact, if you have never used them before, you will have to get used to how little is needed to make beautifully rich-colored dough. Here's how to do it:

Use a toothpick to spread just a nubbin of paste food color on the dough. Knead the color evenly into the dough, dusting your hands with flour if necessary. The color you see when the dough is thoroughly kneaded with the paste is very close to the color it will be when the dough dries; add more paste for a more intense color or more dough to lighten the color.

Wrap each color of dough separately in plastic.

WORKING WITH BREAD/GLUE DOUGH

Gather the basic equipment together, along with any special items mentioned in the *Materials* column. Dust your work surface with flour and follow the instructions for the project you have chosen. **NOTE:** Before you begin, be sure to brush up on the general techniques for working with dough (pages 10–13). Here are two tips to remember:

1. If the fronts (or the backs, especially of ornaments) are dusty-looking from the flour used when you rolled out the dough, brush the newly made item lightly with water to make the flour disappear. The item will dry without that floury look.

2. Rolled-out bread/glue dough can be cut with scissors. For example, outline a template on some rolled-out dough, remove the template and instead of cutting with a knife simply pick up the piece of dough and cut on the outline with small, sharp scissors.

BEFORE DRYING: ATTACHING THE PARTS

While the dough is still moist, the parts of an ornament can be attached using water as the glue. Apply water sparingly with your finger or a small brush and press the pieces together gently but firmly.

BEFORE DRYING: DECORATING THE BREAD/GLUE DOUGH

1. Incising: The dough is quite receptive to all kinds of marking and poking. You can incise a pattern or a mark with the blunt and/or pointed ends of a wooden skewer, the end of a straw, the back of a knife blade or just about anything else. Incising must be done firmly, without going all the way through the dough, and it must be done before the surface of the dough begins to dry.

2. Adding shapes: Leaves, berries, facial features, diamonds, hearts and other dough shapes can be added to a dough ornament

or other dough project with just a bit of water acting as glue. Read the section above, called *Before drying: Attaching the parts*.

3. Adding garlic press strands: The fleece of the sheep and lambs (page 124) and Santa's beard and moustache (page 49) are made by forcing a piece of dough through a garlic press. Force the dough through only until the strands are the length you want. Remove a group of strands by drawing a sharp knife along the base of the strands, or remove a few strands at a time with a toothpick or wooden skewer. Brush water on the project and place the strands in position. Be sure to wash the garlic press carefully before leftover dough dries on it; dried dough is almost impossible to remove.

BEFORE DRYING: MAKING HOLES AND ADDING PAPER CLIP LOOPS

Many of the ornaments require either holes or paper clip loops through which you can thread ribbon or cord for tying the ornament to the Christmas tree. General instructions for making the holes and loops are given in Technique #8 on page 13.

DRYING THE DOUGH

When each project or ornament is completed, transfer it carefully to a piece of waxed paper on a flat surface to air-dry for several hours and then to a wire rack to finish drying. Small pieces dry quickly, but large, flat pieces and very three-dimensional ones will take overnight or even a few days to dry thoroughly. The piece is dry when it feels hard, rigid and not at all damp, with no dark patches. Follow the guidelines below for successful drying.

Flat pieces: Leave on waxed paper for several hours; the edges will begin to curl up. Turn each piece over, let it dry for

several more hours and then transfer it to a wire rack to finish drying. It should dry completely flat.

Three-dimensional and layered pieces: Leave on waxed paper on a flat surface until the top surfaces are dry enough to be turned over without being dented or injured. Turn each piece over, allow it to dry for several more hours and then transfer it to a wire rack to finish drying. Watch layered pieces carefully; if they begin to curl, put them back on the waxed paper until they flatten out again.

Roses and other extremely dimensional pieces: Leave on waxed paper until the tops are quite dry. Then transfer the pieces to a wire rack without turning over and leave there until thoroughly dry.

NOTE: If any parts come off or break apart during the drying process, they can be glued back onto the piece when it is completely dry. Do not try to attach with water.

AFTER DRYING: ATTACHING THE PARTS

Some projects require the various parts to be dried separately and then glued together or glued to some other surface. The individual project will list the kind of glue needed and have instructions for using the glue in that specific situation.

FINISHING THE PIECES

It is not necessary to seal dry bread/glue dough with polyurethane; if you want to seal it to give it a slight sheen or a high gloss, brush it with several coats of satin- or gloss-finish polyurethane, allowing each coat to dry thoroughly before applying the next. After polyurethaning, clean your brush first in turpentine and then with cold water and ordinary hand soap.

Cornstarch dough

This dough, made from cornstarch and baking soda, is very different from the two previous doughs. It is not as versatile, since you cannot make large items with it, but it has its own virtues: Finished items have a beautiful matte finish, almost like unglazed china. The uncolored dough air-dries to a lovely crisp white, but the dough is also particularly pretty when worked in pastel colors. Although it feels quite hard, the dry dough will shatter if dropped; handle it carefully and store cornstarch dough ornaments in lots of tissue paper.

Stir the ingredients together in a saucepan and cook them over medium heat, stirring constantly, until the mixture thickens to a doughlike consistency. Turn the dough out onto a board or other work surface and let it cool enough for you to handle it. Knead the dough for a minute or two. (The dough should still be very warm, so be careful.) Leave the ball of dough on the board, covered with a damp cloth, until it is completely cool. Wrap tightly in plastic or put in a plastic bag secured with a twist tie.

DOS AND DON'TS

Do keep all pieces of dough not in use wrapped tightly in plastic.

Don't store the dough in the refrigerator. It will keep for several weeks unrefrigerated.

Do reknead it for a few minutes if it has been set aside for more than a day.

Don't eat the dough!

PROBLEM-SOLVING: TOO DRY OR TOO MOIST

The dough will begin to dry out if it is exposed to air for a while; knead in a few drops of water to combat the dryness. If it seems too sticky, sprinkle the dough with a little cornstarch and knead it in.

BASIC EQUIPMENT

The list below tells what equipment you will need for working with cornstarch dough; these items are not generally listed in the *Materials* column because I assume you have them handy.

- Tracing paper, carbon paper and thin cardboard for making templates
- Rolling pin
- 2 strips of wood, each 1/8" thick. (See page 11, Technique #1.)
- Waxed paper
- Small spatula; long spatula
- Round wooden toothpicks
- Plastic drinking straws for making holes
- Small brush for applying water to dough

Anything else needed for a specific project will be listed in the *Materials* column—cookie cutters, trims, glue, ribbon and so on.

COLORING THE DOUGH

As with bread/glue dough, cornstarch dough should be tinted with paste food colors before you begin to work with the dough. Buy little jars of red, blue, green and yellow paste food colors; they are

INGREDIENTS

1 cup cornstarch
2 cups baking soda
1¼ cups water

inexpensive and will last a long time because the colors are highly concentrated.

Break off a piece of dough and use a toothpick to smear just a little bit of paste food color on the dough. Work the color into the dough, kneading until the color is evenly distributed, with no streaks. Dust your hands with cornstarch if the dough becomes sticky. Adjust the color, if necessary, by adding more paste for a darker color or more dough to lighten the color. **NOTE:** The dry dough will be a slightly lighter color than the moist dough.

Wrap each color separately in plastic.

WORKING WITH CORNSTARCH DOUGH

Gather the basic equipment together, along with any special items mentioned in the *Materials* column. Dust your work surface with cornstarch and follow the instructions for the project you have chosen. **NOTE:** Before you begin, be sure to brush up on the general techniques for working with dough (pages 10–13). Here are three tips for working with cornstarch dough:

1. Don't roll the dough thinner or much thicker than ⅛" thick; it either becomes too fragile and cracks or it warps severely and splits.

2. Keep your work surface, fingers and cutting tools clean and free of caked, dry bits of dough. The bits on your fingers find their way into the dough to make lumps and the bits on the knife cause ragged cut edges.

3. Any cornstarch dough ornaments you invent should be on the small side, no larger than the white duck (page 54) or the snowflake (page 53).

BEFORE DRYING: ATTACHING THE PARTS

While the dough is still moist, the parts of an ornament can be attached using water as the glue. Apply water sparingly with your finger or a small brush and press the pieces together gently but firmly.

BEFORE DRYING: MAKING HOLES AND ADDING PAPER CLIP LOOPS

Most ornaments made of cornstarch dough require either holes or paper clip loops through which you can thread ribbon for tying the ornament to the Christmas tree. General instructions for making the holes and loops are given in Technique #8 on page 13.

DRYING THE DOUGH

Unless otherwise specified, cornstarch dough ornaments are allowed to air-dry on waxed paper; they must be turned over every few hours (or more often) so they dry flat. You will see that the edges dry first and begin to curl upward—that's the time to turn the ornaments over. They'll dry a little more and begin to curl in the opposite direction—turn them over again. Eventually they will dry to complete hardness, with no damp patches. Tiny pieces may dry very quickly, within an hour or two, while larger ones may take a day or two.

AFTER DRYING: ATTACHING THE PARTS

Some projects require various parts to be dried separately and then glued together. The individual project will list the kind of glue needed and have instructions for using the glue in that specific situation.

Cookie dough

Here is a basic sugar cookie dough, easy to work with and perfect for making decorated Christmas cookies and other Christmas cookie projects.

Cream the margarine and sugar until fluffy. Add the vanilla extract and milk and blend well. Add the flour gradually, mixing after each addition. As the dough gets stiff, you may find it easier to mix with your hands. Divide the dough in half, wrap each half snugly in plastic and chill for two hours or until firm enough to roll out.

Dust the work surface and rolling pin with flour. Follow the instructions for each project for rolling out and cutting the dough.

Bake for 8–10 minutes or as long as the individual project specifies. Let the cookies cool for a few minutes on the cookie sheet and then transfer them to wire racks to finish cooling.

INGREDIENTS

1 cup margarine

1 cup sugar

1 teaspoon vanilla extract

2 tablespoons milk

2½ cups all-purpose flour

Preheat oven to 375°

Baking pan: ungreased cookie sheet or jelly roll pan

Gingerbread dough

This good, spicy gingerbread dough makes delicious cookies and is sturdy enough for gingerbread houses, too.

Cream the margarine, brown sugar and molasses. Add the egg and blend well. Stir together 2½ cups of flour, the baking soda and the spices. Add to the creamed mixture and blend well. If the dough seems very sticky, gradually add the remaining ½ cup of flour until the dough is smooth.

Divide the dough in half, wrap each half snugly in plastic and refrigerate for two hours or until the dough is firm enough to roll out.

Dust the work surface and rolling pin with flour. Follow the instructions for each project for rolling and cutting the dough.

Bake for 8–10 minutes or as long as the individual project specifies. Let the cookies cool for a few minutes on the cookie sheet and then transfer them to wire racks to finish cooling.

INGREDIENTS

½ cup margarine

½ cup dark brown sugar, packed

½ cup molasses

1 egg

2½–3 cups all-purpose flour

1½ teaspoons baking soda

½ teaspoon salt

1½ teaspoons cinnamon

1 teaspoon ginger

½ teaspoon ground cloves

Preheat oven to 350°

Baking pan: ungreased cookie sheet or jelly roll pan

BASIC EQUIPMENT

The list below tells what equipment you will need for working with cookie dough or gingerbread dough; these items are not generally listed in the *Materials* column because I assume you have them handy.

- Tracing paper, carbon paper and thin cardboard for making templates
- Rolling pin
- Heavy-duty cookie sheets or jelly roll pans

NOTE: Cookies can be baked on the back of a jelly roll pan; this is especially convenient when you don't have a second cookie sheet.

- Small spatula; long spatula
- Sharp knife
- Ruler
- Kitchen timer
- Wire racks

Anything else needed for a specific project will be listed in the *Materials* column—cookie cutters, icing, candies and so on.

WORKING WITH COOKIE OR GINGERBREAD DOUGH

Before you begin working with either dough, read pages 10–13 to brush up on general doughcraft techniques. Here are some additional hints and tips to help you:

1. The dough *must* be chilled before you roll it out; warm dough will be very sticky and difficult to roll and to cut. Dough that is too cold is equally hard to work, so don't leave it in the refrigerator too long.

2. One of the best ways to work these doughs is to roll and cut them on the *back* of a jelly roll pan. For some projects this is essential and you will be instructed to do so, but you can do it for any project you wish. The advantage is that dough rolled out directly on the back of the pan can be put back in the refrigerator to chill for a few minutes before and during the process of cutting with a template or cookie cutter. This gives you crisper cuts with less stickiness.

3. Use a sharp (not serrated) knife for cutting around templates and wipe the blade often with a damp paper towel. Dipping the blade in flour is helpful with sticky dough, too.

4. Dip cookie cutters in flour before pressing them into the dough. Wipe the cutting edge if it becomes caked with dough.

5. Don't cut around the template and then try to remove the excess dough; remove excess dough *as you cut*.

6. Gather up excess dough and knead it into a smooth ball. Shape the ball into a thick, flat rectangle, wrap tightly in plastic and return to the refrigerator to chill.

7. As extra flour is incorporated into the dough during rolling, the dough gets easier to work with—but the cookies will be a bit tougher when they are baked.

8. Let cookies cool on the cookie sheet for a few minutes before you try to move them to wire racks to finish cooling. Cookies are soft and flexible when they are very hot, and a large cookie (like the engine of the Cookie Train, page 129) will bend and break before you can get it from the cookie sheet to the wire rack.

Decorator icing

This basic icing is used for piping and painting decorations on cookie and gingerbread projects and for gluing cookies together. You will find it is quite easy to work with. It mixes beautifully with food coloring (especially paste food colors), lasts for several days in the refrigerator and dries hard and crisp.

Put the ingredients in a deep bowl and beat with an electric mixer at high speed for five minutes, scraping down the sides occasionally. Cover the finished icing with a piece of plastic wrap placed directly on the icing.

COLORING THE ICING

Ordinary liquid food color is perfectly adequate for tinting the icing if you want ordinary pastel colors. For really bright, intense colors (like Christmas red and green, sunny yellow and rich blue) as well as prettier, clearer pastels, you must use paste food colors.

Paste food colors (thick, concentrated colors that come in little jars) are available wherever cake-decorating supplies are sold. They are economical to use, since a small amount goes a very long way. A basic palette of red, green, yellow, blue and brown (plus orange and violet if you like) will last for years.

To color the icing, first divide it into several small bowls, one bowl for each color. **NOTE:** Leave one bowl of icing white. Cover each bowl with a piece of plastic wrap placed directly on the icing.

Begin with one bowl: Uncover the icing and use a toothpick to put a small bit of paste food color in the bowl. Mix briskly with a spoon to distribute the color evenly. Adjust the color if necessary by adding more paste food color to make it darker or brighter or adding more icing to lighten it. When you have the color you want, recover with plastic wrap and repeat the process to make the other colors you need.

INGREDIENTS

3½ cups (1 pound) confectioners' sugar

¾ teaspoon cream of tartar

3 egg whites

½ teaspoon vanilla extract

¼ teaspoon almond extract

A SHORT LESSON ON PIPING

If you've never done any piping, you are probably convinced that it is something best left to the magic-fingered professionals. Believe me, it's not. Anyone can do it. Your piping may never be as gorgeous as the pros', but so what? It's tremendous fun and you *will* get better and better at it. Just buy the right equipment, use the right icing (recipe above) and practice not until you're perfect but just until you're having a good time. The *Materials* list tells you what you'll need to start.

It is much easier to do piping if you have several decorating bags—one for each color is ideal—plus the couplers and plenty of icing tips, but you can start with

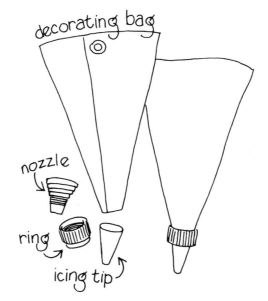

decorating bag

nozzle

ring

icing tip

MATERIALS

1 recipe of decorator icing

1 decorating bag (sometimes called a pastry bag), 10″ long, made of plastic-lined muslin

1 plastic coupler, consisting of a nozzle and a threaded ring for connecting the icing tip to the decorating bag

#2 icing tip

Small spatula

Waxed paper

just one set. Begin by putting together the decorating bag, coupler and icing tip, following the manufacturer's instructions included with the coupler.

To fill the decorating bag with icing, fold the bag down over your hand to form a cuff, as shown in the drawing. Hold the bag open and use the small spatula to fill it half-full of icing. Fold the cuff back up, fold the sides in and roll the end down.

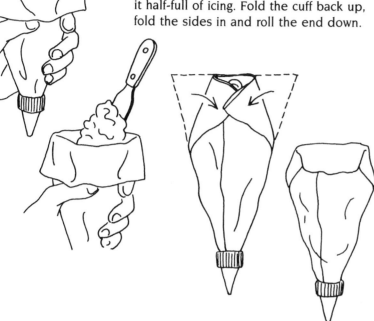

Grasp the folded end of the bag with one hand; with your other hand you will squeeze out the icing in a smooth flow and guide the tip at the same time.

You are ready to begin practicing on a piece of waxed paper. Try a few straight lines: Hold the bag at about a 30° angle to the paper. Squeeze out the icing smoothly and steadily with one hand while you move your other hand to make the line. The tip should just barely touch the surface of the paper without digging in or dragging. Practice until you feel comfortable.

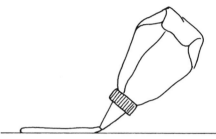

Now try some dots: Hold the bag perpendicular to the paper with the tip just touching the surface. Squeeze out a little icing. When the icing forms a tiny mound, stop squeezing, lift up and move the tip away in a smooth motion. Make a whole row of dots.

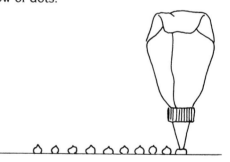

When you're in the swing of it, go on to make some scallops, loops, wavy lines and a few rings of dots. Finally, pipe some faces, bow ties, curlicues and a few very simple letters and numbers.

If the project you have chosen requires other icing tips, it's a good idea to practice with them for a while, too.

STORING THE ICING

Leftover icing can be stored in the refrigerator for several days. If it is in a bowl, be sure the plastic wrap lies directly on the icing, covering it completely so it won't form a crust. When you take it out of the refrigerator, stir it briskly with a fork before using. If it is in a decorating bag, first remove the icing tip and wash it. Cover the exposed plastic nozzle with a bit of plastic wrap and secure the wrap with a rubber band. When you take it out of the refrigerator, reattach the tip and go to work.

FINAL NOTE

This icing is also used as glue when you are putting two cookies together (see the Cookie Train, page 129), adhering a small cookie to a larger one (see the Gingerbread Christmas Tree, page 138) or attaching little candies to cookies or gingerbread (see the Little Gingerbread House Favors, page 110).

Whatever your taste, whatever your style, there's a doughcraft ornament (or seven or eight ornaments) for you. If you cozy up to a country style, try the cottages, baskets, farm animals and little redware plates shown on the tree on page 64. If you swoon over the romantic look, there are charming flower ornaments for you on the tree on page 58. If red, white and green mean Christmas to you, you'll love the ornaments on page 52. If you like all things Christmasy, make one of each. There are dozens of ornaments from which to choose.

Most of the instructions are written for making one of each ornament, but of course you will want to make multiples of each one you love. One batch of the requisite dough will be enough to make at least several of any ornament.

Simple Coil Wreath

MATERIALS

Flour/salt dough (page 16)

Paste food color (brown)

Acrylic paint (red), brush

Polyurethane, brush, turpentine

Sobo glue

Satin ribbon, ¼″ wide, one piece 20″ long

The instructions are for making one ornament.

Photograph, page 32, for design and color guidance

1. Make the basic wreath.

Use paste food color to tint some dough light brown. Roll a rope 22″–23″ long and ¼″ in diameter and transfer it to a cookie sheet or the back of a jelly roll pan. Shape the rope into a wreath, forming the coils as shown in the drawing. Complete the wreath by cutting off any excess rope and joining the end of the rope to the beginning of the rope with a dab of water. Smooth the two ends together.

2. Make the berries.

Roll 20 little balls of uncolored dough, each ¼″ in diameter. Place them on the cookie sheet. **NOTE:** Make 20 berries in order to wind up with eight good ones because some of the berries will crack during baking.

3. Bake the wreath and berries.

Bake at 250° for 15 minutes. If the berries are done at this point, remove them; if not, bake a few more minutes and then take them out of the oven. Turn the wreath over. Continue baking for 15 more minutes or until completely hard. Remove the wreath from the oven and allow it to cool.

4. Paint the berries and polyurethane the wreath.

Paint eight perfect (not cracked) berries with two coats of red, letting each coat dry thoroughly.

Paint the wreath with one coat of polyurethane and let it dry.

5. Glue the berries to the wreath and finish the wreath.

One side of the wreath will be flatter than the other; that side is the right side. Glue each berry in place on the right side of the wreath: Pick up each berry with tweezers, dip it in glue and put it in position as shown in the drawing. Let the glue dry.

Brush another coat of polyurethane on the wreath *and* on the berries; this helps to anchor the berries to the wreath as well as seal the whole ornament. Let the polyurethane dry thoroughly.

6. Add the ribbon.

Fold the ribbon in half and push the ribbon loop up through one of the dough loops. Slip the ends of the ribbon through the ribbon loop and pull them tight (Method #1, page 14). Tie the wreath to the tree, making a pretty bow.

Folk Art Ornaments: Round

This ornament and the three following have a cozy folk art style reminiscent of Scandinavia. You might like to combine all four varieties with white lights and red and green shiny balls on your Christmas tree.

The instructions are for making one ornament.

Photograph, page 32, for design and color guidance

1. Make the basic round.

Roll out some dough to ¼" thick. Use the cookie cutter to cut a round. Transfer it to a cookie sheet. Crimp the edge firmly with a fork; be careful not to cut all the way through the dough.

Use the wire cutter to make a paper clip loop; insert the loop in the round. (See page 13 for more information about paper clip loops.)

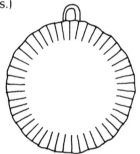

Brush the front of the round with light brown glaze.

2. Bake the round.

Bake at 250° for 15 minutes and then run a spatula under the round to loosen it from the cookie sheet. Bake for another 15 minutes, transfer the round, right side up, to a wire rack and continue baking until the round is completely hard. Remove from the oven and allow to cool.

3. Paint and polyurethane the round.

Paint two coats of red on the back, the edge and a little bit of the front to make a border as shown. Let each coat dry thoroughly.

Now paint the dots and lines on the front, following the step-by-step diagram. Let the paint dry.

Brush two or three coats of polyurethane on the round, letting each coat dry before applying the next.

4. Add the ribbon.

Fold the grosgrain ribbon in half and push the ribbon loop up through the paper clip loop. Slip the ends of the ribbon through the ribbon loop and pull them tight (Method #1, page 14). Tie to the tree, making a pretty bow.

MATERIALS

Flour/salt dough (page 16)

Round cookie cutter, about 2¾" in diameter

Fork

Paper clip (regular size), wire cutter

Light brown glaze (page 21)

Acrylic paints (red, green, white); brushes

Polyurethane, brush, turpentine

Grosgrain ribbon, ¼" wide, one piece 20" long

Folk Art Ornaments: Heart

MATERIALS

Flour/salt dough (page 16)

Heart cookie cutter, about 2¾″ wide

Fork

Paper clip (regular size), wire cutter

Light brown glaze (page 21)

Acrylic paints (red, green, white); brushes

Polyurethane, brush, turpentine

Grosgrain ribbon, ¼″ wide, one piece 20″ long

The instructions are for making one ornament.

Photograph, page 32, for design and color guidance

1. Make the basic heart.

Roll out some dough to ¼″ thick. Use the cookie cutter to cut a heart. Transfer it to a cookie sheet. Crimp the edge of the heart firmly with a fork; be careful not to cut all the way through the dough.

Use the wire cutter to cut a paper clip loop; insert the loop in the heart. (See page 13 for more information about paper clip loops.)

Brush the front of the heart with light brown glaze.

2. Bake the heart.

Bake at 250° for 15 minutes and then run a spatula under the heart to loosen it from the cookie sheet. Bake for another 15 minutes, transfer the heart, right side up, to a wire rack and continue baking until the heart is completely hard. Remove from the oven and allow to cool.

3. Paint and polyurethane the heart.

Paint two coats of red on the back, the edge and a little bit of the front to make a border as shown. Let each coat dry thoroughly.

Now paint the dots and lines on the front, following the step-by-step diagram. Let the paint dry.

Brush two or three coats of polyurethane on the heart, letting each coat dry before applying the next.

4. Add the ribbon.

Fold the grosgrain ribbon in half and push the ribbon loop up through the paper clip loop. Slip the ends of the ribbon through the ribbon loop and pull them tight (Method #1, page 14). Tie to the tree, making a pretty bow.

Folk Art Ornaments: Reindeer

The instructions are for making one ornament.

Photograph, page 32, for design and color guidance

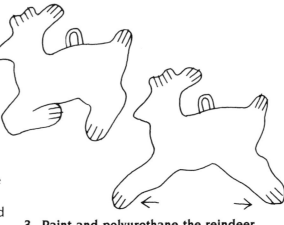

1. Make the basic reindeer.

Roll out some dough to ¼" thick. Use the cookie cutter to cut a reindeer. Transfer it to a cookie sheet. If the reindeer has folded legs, either leave them as they are or extend them as shown in the drawing. Use the fork to crimp the feet, the tail and the tips of the antlers.

Use the wire cutter to make a paper clip loop; insert the loop in the reindeer. (See page 13 for more information about paper clip loops.)

Brush the front of the reindeer with light brown glaze.

2. Bake the reindeer.

Bake at 250° for 15 minutes and then run a spatula under the reindeer to loosen it from the cookie sheet. Bake for another 15 minutes, transfer the reindeer, right side up, to a wire rack and continue baking until the reindeer is completely hard. Remove from the oven and allow to cool.

3. Paint and polyurethane the reindeer.

Paint two coats of red on the back, the edge and a little bit of the front to make a border as shown. Let each coat dry thoroughly.

Now paint the dots and lines on the front, following the diagram. Let the paint dry.

Brush two or three coats of polyurethane on the reindeer, letting each coat dry before applying the next.

4. Add the ribbon.

Fold the grosgrain ribbon in half and push the ribbon loop up through the paper clip loop. Slip the ends of the ribbon through the ribbon loop and pull them tight (Method #1, page 14). Tie to the tree, making a pretty bow.

MATERIALS

Flour/salt dough (page 16)

Reindeer cookie cutter

Fork

Paper clip (regular size), wire cutter

Light brown glaze (page 21)

Acrylic paints (red, green, white); brushes

Polyurethane, brush, turpentine

Grosgrain ribbon, ¼" wide, one piece 20" long

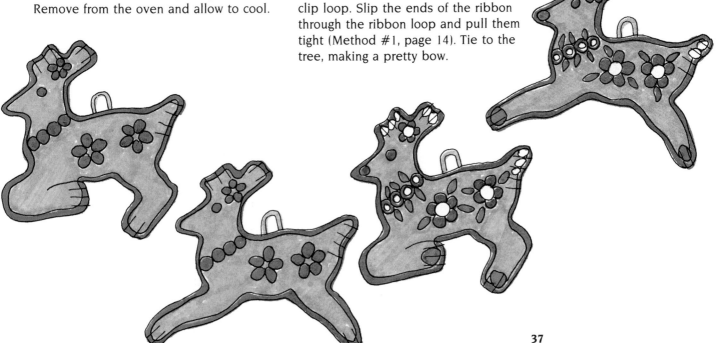

Folk Art Ornaments: Christmas Tree

Photograph, page 32, for design and color guidance

MATERIALS

Flour/salt dough (page 16)

Christmas tree cookie cutter

Fork

Paper clip (regular size), wire cutter

Light brown glaze (page 21)

Acrylic paints (red, green, white); brushes

Polyurethane, brush, turpentine

Grosgrain ribbon, ¼″ wide, one piece 20″ long

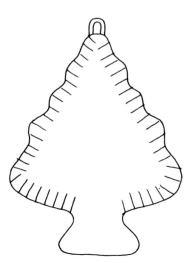

The instructions are for making one ornament.

Photograph, page 32, for design and color guidance

1. Make the basic tree.

Roll out some dough to ¼″ thick. Use the cookie cutter to cut a tree. Transfer it to a cookie sheet. Crimp the edge of the tree (but not the trunk) firmly with a fork; be careful not to cut all the way through the dough.

Use the wire cutter to make a paper clip loop; insert the loop in the tree. (See page 13 for more information about paper clip loops.)

Brush the front of the tree with light brown glaze.

2. Bake the tree.

Bake at 250° for 15 minutes and then run a spatula under the tree to loosen it from the cookie sheet. Bake for another 15 minutes, transfer the tree, right side up, to a wire rack and continue baking until the tree is completely hard. Remove from the oven and allow to cool.

3. Paint and polyurethane the tree.

Paint two coats of red on the back, the edge and a little bit of the front to make a border as shown. Let each coat dry thoroughly.

Now paint the dots and lines on the front, following the step-by-step diagram. Let the paint dry.

Brush two or three coats of polyurethane on the tree, letting each coat dry before applying the next.

4. Add the ribbon.

Fold the grosgrain ribbon in half and push the ribbon loop up through the paper clip loop. Slip the ends of the ribbon through the ribbon loop and pull them tight (Method #1, page 14). Tie to the actual Christmas tree, making a pretty bow.

Flower Coin Garland

Photograph, page 32, for design and color guidance

1. Make the basic coins.

Roll out half of the dough to ⅛" thick. Use the cookie cutter to cut as many rounds as possible from the rolled dough. Make a hole in the center of each round with a narrow plastic straw. Place the coins on waxed paper to dry. Repeat with the remaining dough.

Turn the coins over every few hours so they dry flat.

2. Decorate the coins.

When the coins are completely dry, decorate each one with felt-tip markers: Draw eight red petals on each side of the coin and then make a line of green on the edge of the coin, referring to the drawing below for guidance.

3. Join the coins with yarn.

Instead of making one garland, make several shorter ones. To make one short garland, start with an eight-foot piece of yarn.

Slip a coin onto the yarn and push it to the middle. Tie a double knot. Now work out toward each end, tying a coin about every 2½"-3". Leave 8"-10" of yarn free at each end. **NOTE:** If you have trouble threading the yarn through the holes in the coins, smear a little Sobo glue on the end of the yarn, roll the end between your fingers to compress and stiffen it, and let the glue dry.

Repeat to make more garlands.

MATERIALS

Cornstarch dough (page 25)

Round cookie cutter, 1" in diameter

Bright red felt-tip marker with medium-pointed nib (not fine-pointed)

Bright green felt-tip marker with medium-pointed nib (not fine-pointed)

Red yarn, 4-ply or worsted-weight

Flying Angels

Make angels with pink skin and brown skin. Alter the color of the dress, dress trim and eyes as indicated; colors are for the pink-skinned angel, with changes for the brown-skinned angel in parentheses.

The instructions are for making one ornament.

Photograph, page 40, for design and color guidance

1. Color the dough.

For the pink-skinned angel you will need small amounts of white (uncolored), pink, yellow, green, light brown and a pinch of blue dough. You will also need a slightly larger amount of red.

For the brown-skinned angel you will need small amounts of white (uncolored), light brown, yellow, red and dark brown dough. You will also need a slightly larger amount of light blue.

2. Make the basic body.

Transfer the dress and wing patterns to thin cardboard to make templates as explained on page 12.

Dress: Roll some red (light blue) dough to ⅛″ thick. Place the dress template on the dough, hold it lightly and outline it with the pointed tip of a knife. Cut out the dress with scissors and place it on a piece of waxed paper.

MATERIALS

Bread/glue dough (page 22)

Paste food colors (red, yellow, green, brown, blue)

Fluted pastry wheel

Garlic press

Gold soutache, one piece 20″ long

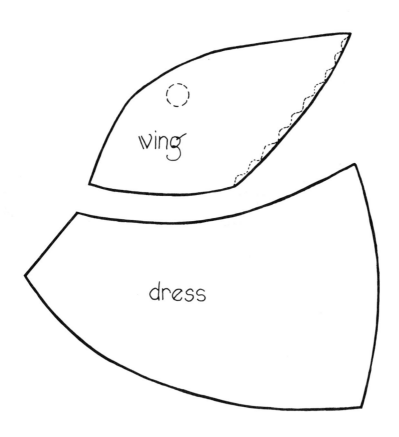

Head: Roll a ball of pink (light brown) dough ¾″ in diameter. Flatten it to be about 1⅛″ in diameter. Flatten the neck edge of the dress, brush with water and press the head in place on the flattened edge.

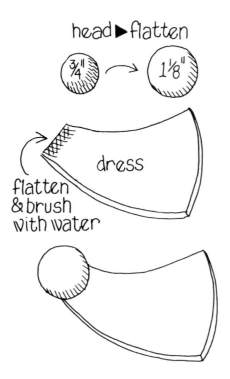

Sleeve and hand: Roll some red (light blue) dough into a rope ⅜″ in diameter and about 1¾″ long. Flatten it slightly and shape the hand end straight and the shoulder end rounded. Roll a little pink (light brown) ball, flatten one side and brush the flattened part with water. Tuck the flattened side under the sleeve and press gently to adhere. Brush water on the back of the sleeve and hand and gently press into position on the dress.

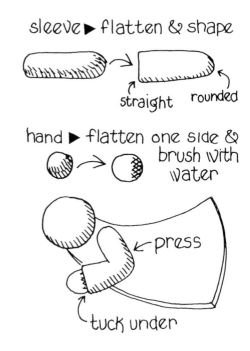

Feet: Roll two little yellow ovals. Flatten one end of each oval, brush with water and tuck under the dress. Press the dress gently onto the ovals to adhere them.

3. Add the wing.
Roll out some white dough to ⅛″ thick. Place the wing template on the dough, hold it lightly and outline it with the pointed tip of a knife. Cut out two sides with scissors and use the fluted pastry wheel to cut the third side, as shown.

Flatten the lower edge of the wing and brush with water. Tuck it under the top edge of the dress and press lightly to adhere.

Use a plastic straw to make a hole in the wing.

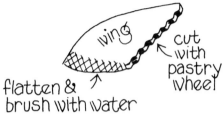

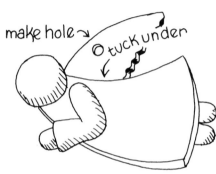

4. Add the halo, dress trim, hair and facial features.

Halo: Roll some yellow dough into a rope ¼" in diameter and about 3" long. Join the ends with a dab of water to form a ring. Flatten the ring as shown, brush with water and tuck under the head. Press the head gently onto the halo to adhere.

Dress trim: Roll two very thin green (red) ropes, each about 3¼" long. Brush water onto the lower edge of the dress and place each rope in position, shaping it in a wavy line. (See photograph, page 40.) Cut off any excess rope. Press the ropes lightly to adhere them to the dress.

Hair: Press a small ball of light brown (dark brown) dough through a garlic press until the strands are about ½" long. Brush water around the angel's face and head. Use a

toothpick to remove two or three strands of dough at a time from the garlic press; place the strands in position around the face, pressing gently to adhere them.

Facial features: Roll two tiny balls of blue (dark brown) dough for the eyes, a tiny red ball for the nose and a tiny red rope for the smile. Brush water on the face and press each feature in position.

Let the angel dry for several hours on the waxed paper, until the figure is stiff enough to be transferred to a wire rack to finish drying. Depending on the temperature and humidity, this may take more than several hours. Do not lift or move a floppy angel because the wing and/or head could easily break off.

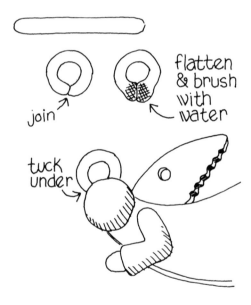

5. Add the soutache.

Fold a 20"-long piece of braid in half and push the loop up through the hole in the angel's wing. Slip the ends of the braid through the loop and pull them tight (Method #1, page 14). Tie to the tree, making a pretty bow.

Dough Pretzel

MATERIALS

Flour/salt dough (page 16)

Acrylic paints (white, assorted colors); brushes

Polyurethane, brush, turpentine

Grosgrain ribbon, ⅜" wide, one piece 18" long

These ornaments are especially easy and fun for kids to make. The instructions are for making one pretzel.

Photograph, page 40, for design and color guidance

1. Make the basic pretzel.

Roll a piece of dough into a rope ½" in diameter and cut off a section 14" long. Transfer the rope to a cookie sheet. Shape it into a pretzel as shown in the drawing, dabbing water on the dough at the overlaps. Round off the cut ends with dampened fingers.

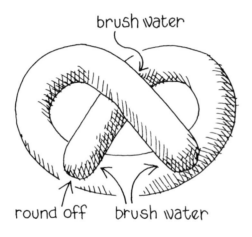

brush water

round off   brush water

2. Bake the basic pretzel.

Bake at 250° for about half an hour and then run a spatula under the pretzel to loosen it from the cookie sheet. Continue baking, without turning, until completely hard. Remove from the oven and allow to cool.

3. Paint and polyurethane the pretzel.

Paint one coat of white on the pretzel and let it dry. Next paint polka dots all over the pretzel, checking the photograph on page 40 for ideas about color. When the dots are dry, paint the remaining white background with two coats of a bright, contrasting color. Now go back and paint a second coat of color on each polka dot. Let the paint dry thoroughly.

Brush two or three coats of polyurethane on the pretzel, letting each coat dry before applying the next.

4. Add the ribbon.

Tie each end of the ribbon around the pretzel, making double knots as shown in the photograph on page 40. Trim the ends of the ribbon on the diagonal.

Golden Star with Sequins

The instructions are for making one ornament.

Photograph, page 40, for design and color guidance

1. Make the basic star.
Transfer the pattern to thin cardboard to make a template as explained on page 12.

Roll out some dough to ¼" thick. Place the template on the dough, hold it lightly and cut around it, removing the excess dough as you cut.

Carefully lift the star on a wide spatula and place it on a cookie sheet. Straighten out the points if necessary.

2. Bake the star.
Bake at 250° for 15 minutes and then turn over. Bake for 15 more minutes or until completely hard.

3. Paint and polyurethane the star.
Paint the star with one coat of white and then two coats of gold, letting each coat dry before applying the next.

Brush on two or three coats of polyurethane, letting each coat dry thoroughly.

4. Apply the sequins to the star.
Cement sequins to the star, following the drawing or inventing your own design.

5. Add the soutache.
Fold the soutache in half and cement the ends to the back of one point of the star (Method #2, page 14). Let the cement dry completely before hanging the star on the tree.

MATERIALS

Flour/salt dough (page 16)

Acrylic paint (white, opaque gold); brush

Polyurethane, brush, turpentine

8mm sequins (red, green, blue, amber, magenta)

Gold soutache, one piece 5" long

527 cement

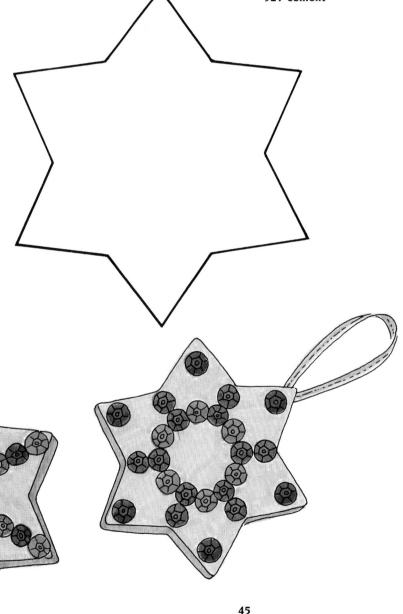

Golden Star with Gold Trim

MATERIALS

Flour/salt dough (page 16)

2 star cookie cutters, one about 2¾″ wide and one about 1½″ wide

Acrylic paint (white, opaque gold); brush

Polyurethane, brush, turpentine

**Gold trim, one piece about 12″ long
NOTE: Choose a flexible trim with a narrow heading.**

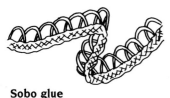

Sobo glue

Gold soutache, one piece 5″ long

527 cement

The instructions are for making one ornament.

Photograph, page 40, for design and color guidance

1. Make the basic star.

Roll out some dough to ⅛″ thick. Use the cookie cutters to cut one large star and one small star. Brush water on the back of the smaller star and center it on the larger star, pressing it gently to adhere the two.

Transfer the basic star to a cookie sheet.

2. Bake the star.

Bake at 250° for about 15 minutes. Turn the star over, bake for ten more minutes and turn again. Continue baking and turning every ten minutes until the star is completely hard.

3. Paint and polyurethane the star.

Paint the star with one coat of white and then two coats of gold, letting each coat dry before applying the next.

Brush on two or three coats of polyurethane, letting each coat dry thoroughly.

4. Apply the gold trim to the back of the star.

Use Sobo glue for attaching the gold trim, applying the glue to the star with a toothpick. Begin gluing on the back of the star at the point indicated in the drawing. Only the heading is actually glued to the back of the star, so just the decorative trim shows from the front. Work around to the beginning, turning the corners carefully. When you arrive back at the starting point, clip off the excess trim and be sure the end is glued down neatly.

Let the glue dry thoroughly.

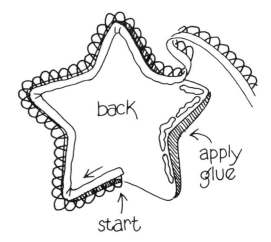

5. Add the soutache.

Fold the soutache in half and use 527 cement to attach the ends to the back of one point of the star (Method #2, page 14). Let the cement dry completely before hanging the star on the tree.

Golden Star with Glitter

The instructions are for making one ornament.

Photograph, page 40, for design and color guidance

1. Make the basic star.

Transfer the pattern to thin cardboard to make a template as explained on page 12.

Roll out some dough to ¼" thick. Place the template on the dough, hold it lightly and cut around it, removing the excess dough as you cut. Carefully lift the star on a wide spatula and place it on a cookie sheet. Straighten out the points if necessary.

2. Bake the star.

Bake at 250° for 15 minutes and then turn the star over. Bake for 15 more minutes or until completely hard.

3. Paint and polyurethane the star.

Paint the star with one coat of white and then two coats of gold, letting each coat dry before applying the next.

Brush on two or three coats of polyurethane, letting each coat dry thoroughly.

MATERIALS

Flour/salt dough (page 16)

Acrylic paint (white, opaque gold); brush

Polyurethane, brush, turpentine

Glitter pens (red, blue, green, gold)

Gold soutache, one piece 5" long

527 cement

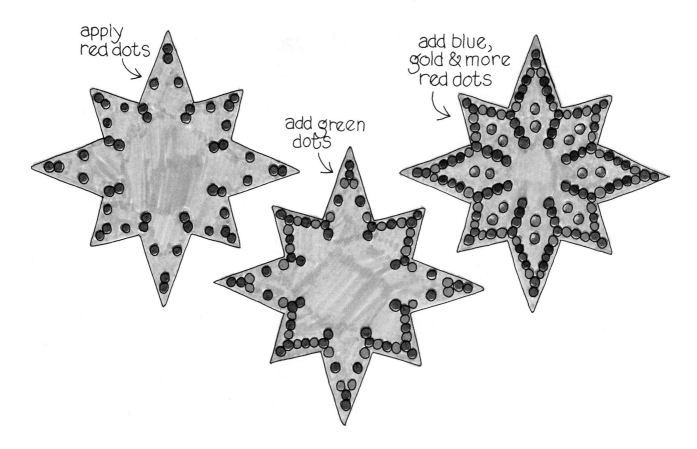

apply
red dots

add green
dots

add blue,
gold & more
red dots

4. Apply the glitter to the star.

Using the glitter pens, apply dots of glitter to the star, following the step-by-step diagram above. Let the glitter dry thoroughly.

5. Add the soutache.

Fold the soutache in half and cement the ends to the back of one long point of the star (Method #2, page 14). Let the cement dry completely before hanging the star on the tree.

Santa Ornament

The instructions are for one ornament, but it is quite easy to make three at a time, once you get the hang of it. This is good, too, because you will have to clean the garlic press only once or twice instead of after making each ornament. It is very important not to let the bread/glue dough (or any other dough) dry in the garlic press; if it does dry, you will never get it all out again.

Photograph, page 40, for design and color guidance

1. Color the dough.

Color a piece of dough (about one third of one recipe) bright green. Color a small piece of dough red, another small piece pink and leave another small piece white (uncolored). Take a little pinch of the white and color it blue. Wrap each color separately in plastic.

2. Make the foundation, the face and part of the hat.

To make the foundation, roll out some green dough to ⅛" thick. Use the scalloped cookie cutter to cut a round and use a plastic straw to make a hole in the round. Place the foundation on a piece of waxed paper.

To make the face, roll a ball of pink dough about 1" in diameter. Flatten it to about 1½" in diameter, making it rounded at the center and flatter at the edges. Pinch up some dough in the center of the round and mold it to make the nose. Use your little finger to make indentations for the eye sockets and the blunt end of a wooden skewer to make holes where the blue eyes will go later.

To make the first part of the hat, roll a ball of red dough ¾" in diameter. Flatten it and shape a hat as shown. Brush water across the top of the face and press the hat over it.

MATERIALS

Bread/glue dough (page 22)

Paste food colors (green, red, blue)

Scalloped cookie cutter, about 2¾" in diameter

Garlic press

Red-and-white gingham ribbon, ⅜" wide, one piece 20" long for each ornament

Brush water on the back of the face and hat and press into position on the foundation as shown. Be sure you don't cover up the hole.

3. Add the details to the face.

Cheeks: Roll two tiny red balls. Brush water on the face and press each ball onto the face, flattening them when you press them in position.

Eyes: Roll two very tiny blue balls. Dot water in the eye sockets and press a blue ball into each one.

Eyebrows, moustache and beard: Force a small piece of white dough through the garlic press until the strands are about ½" long. Brush water above the eyes, under the nose and all around the cheeks and chin.

Use a toothpick to lift and place one strand of dough over each eye to make the eyebrows. Place some short strands of dough under the nose to make the moustache. Poke the ends firmly into the face, making sure the moustache is adhered. Place short strands around the chin and slightly longer strands around the cheeks to make the beard. Again, poke the ends of the strands firmly into the face with the point of a toothpick.

Wash the garlic press immediately with hot water and a stiff brush, so the dough does not dry in the holes.

4. Add the details to the hat.

Roll some white dough into a ball about ⅜″ in diameter. Dab water on the top of the hat and press the ball in place on it.

Roll a small piece of white dough into a rope about ¼″ in diameter and a little longer than the lower edge of the hat. Flatten the rope slightly. Brush water along the lower edge of the hat and press the rope onto the edge. Use the blunt end of a wooden skewer to incise the decorative holes in the white dough.

Let the Santa ornament dry for several hours on the waxed paper, without turning it over. Place the ornament on a wire rack to finish drying. It may take up to several days to dry because of the thickness at the center of the ornament.

5. Add the ribbon.

Fold the gingham ribbon in half and push the loop up through the hole in the ornament. Slip the ends of the ribbon through the loop and pull them tight (Method #1, page 14). Tie to the tree, making a pretty bow.

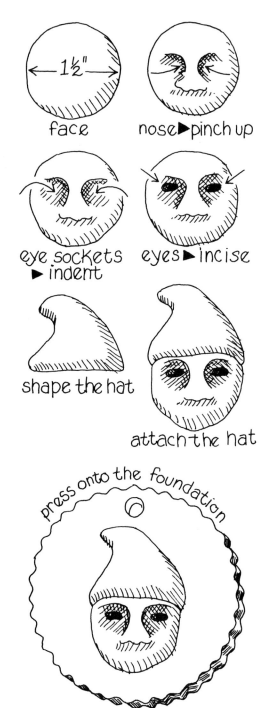

face

nose ▶ pinch up

eye sockets ▶ indent

eyes ▶ incise

shape the hat

attach the hat

press onto the foundation

Silver Bells

The instructions are for making one pair of silver bells.

Photograph, page 40, for design and color guidance

1. Make the basic pair of bells.

Roll out some dough to ⅛" thick. Use the cookie cutter to cut one bell. Roll out some dough to ¼" thick and cut a second bell. Transfer both bells to a cookie sheet.

Use the cookie cutter to cut away a section of the ⅛"-thick bell, as shown in the drawing. Brush water on the newly cut edge and fit the ¼"-thick bell into the cut-out.

Roll two very thin ropes. Brush water on the bells and press the ropes gently into position as shown. Cut off any excess rope. Roll a small ball of dough, flatten it and cut it in half. Use dabs of water to attach one half to each bell to represent the clappers. Use a plastic straw to make a hole in each bell.

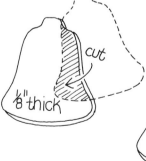

2. Bake the bells.

Bake at 250° for 15 minutes or until the tops of the bells are firm. Turn over and continue baking for 15 more minutes. Turn over again and continue baking until the ornament is completely hard.

3. Paint and polyurethane the bells.

Paint with one coat of white. When the white is dry, paint two coats of silver everywhere except between the thin ropes. Carefully paint two coats of red on each clapper. Let each coat dry before applying the next one.

Brush on two or three coats of polyurethane, letting each coat dry thoroughly.

4. Apply the red and green rickrack to the bells.

Check the drawing to see where the baby rickrack is placed on the bells. Measure and cut two little red pieces and two little green pieces. Use a toothpick to apply glue either to the back of each piece of rickrack or directly onto the bells; press each piece of rickrack in place. **NOTE:** Tweezers are very helpful for picking up and moving the rickrack. Let the glue dry.

5. Add the rickrack loop to the bells.

Thread one end of the 20"-long piece of rickrack up through each of the holes in the bells. Tie the ends in a pretty bow.

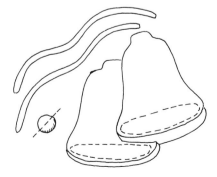

MATERIALS

Flour/salt dough (page 16)

Small bell cookie cutter

Acrylic paints (white, red, opaque silver); brushes

Polyurethane, brush, turpentine

Green baby rickrack, one piece 20" long

Scraps of red and green baby rickrack for the trim

Sobo glue

Snowflake

The instructions are for making one snowflake.

Photograph, page 52, for design and color guidance

1. Make the basic snowflake.

Transfer the pattern to thin cardboard to make a template as explained on page 12.

Roll out the dough to a little more than 1/8" thick. Place the template on the dough, hold it lightly and cut around it with a sharp knife. Be sure to keep the knife blade clean so the edges of the snowflake will be crisp and smooth.

Use the aspic cutter to cut hearts in the snowflake as shown on the pattern. Transfer the snowflake to waxed paper to dry. Turn it often during the drying period so it will dry evenly and flat, without warping or cracking.

2. Add the ribbon.

When the snowflake is dry, bend the ribbon in half and glue the ends to the back, between two hearts. When the glue is completely dry, slide the loop over a branch of your Christmas tree (Method #2, page 14).

MATERIALS
Cornstarch dough (page 25)
Heart-shaped aspic cutter
Satin ribbon, 1/2" wide, one piece 7" long
Sobo glue

White Duck

MATERIALS

Cornstarch dough (page 25)

Satin ribbon, ¼" wide, one piece 8" long for the necktie and one piece 20" long for the loop

The instructions are for making one ornament.

Photograph, page 52, for design and color guidance

1. Make the basic duck.

Transfer the duck and wing patterns to thin cardboard to make a template as explained on page 12.

Roll out the dough to ⅛" thick. Place the duck template and the wing template on the dough, hold each one lightly and cut around it with a sharp knife. Keep the knife blade very clean so the edges of the duck and wing will be crisp and smooth. Use a plastic straw to make a hole in the duck.

Brush a little water both on the duck and on the back of the wing and gently press the wing in position. Roll a tiny ball of dough for the eye, flatten it slightly and press it on the duck with a dot of water.

Place the duck on waxed paper to dry; turn it over every few hours until it is completely dry.

2. Add the ribbon.

Tie the 8"-long piece of ribbon around the duck's neck, making a pretty bow. Fold the 20"-long piece of ribbon in half, push the loop up through the hole and then slip the ends of the ribbon through the loop. Pull the ends tight and tie them to the tree (Method #1, page 14).

Snowfolks

The instructions are for making one snowperson.

Photograph, page 52, for design and color guidance

1. Make the basic snowperson.
Work on a piece of waxed paper.

Roll one ball of dough ¾″ in diameter and another ball 1″ in diameter. Flatten each one so it is rounded in the middle and thinner at the edges; the smaller one will now be about 1⅛″-1¼″ in diameter and the larger one will be about 1¾″ in diameter. Brush water along the top of the larger circle and overlap the smaller one on the water, pressing it gently so it adheres.

2. Add the decorations.
Break off a bit of dough, color it red and shape a little red hat to fit the head of the snowperson. Brush water across the head and press the hat in place. Roll a bit of red dough into a rope and attach it to the hat with water. Use a narrow plastic straw to make a hole. Roll a tiny red rope for the mouth; attach it with water and poke holes with a toothpick.

Break off another bit of white dough and color it bright green. Roll a piece of green to make a rope about ⅛″-¼″ in diameter and 5″ long. Cut the rope in half and use it to make the scarf as shown in the color drawing, attaching it with a little water. Roll three small green balls for the eyes and the pompon. Dot water on the face and hat and press each ball gently in place.

Leave the snowperson on the waxed paper for 12 hours overnight. Then lift

very carefully on a long spatula and transfer to a wire rack so the back can dry, too. Allow the dough to dry thoroughly without moving it again.

3. Add the ribbon.
Thread one end of the ribbon through the hole and tie both ends to the tree, making a pretty bow.

MATERIALS

Cornstarch dough (page 25)

Paste food colors (red, green)

Satin ribbon, ¼″ wide, one piece 20″ long

Striped Ornaments

Photograph, page 52, for design and color guidance

MATERIALS

2 recipes of bread/glue dough (page 22)

Paste food color (red)

Liquid food color (red)

Christmas cookie cutters (star, tree, candy cane, etc.)

Ribbon or flat cord, ⅛" wide, one piece 18" long for each ornament

1. Make a stack of red and white dough rectangles.

Color one recipe of dough bright red, using red paste food color plus a few drops of liquid red food color. **NOTE:** The liquid has a pink tone and the paste has an orange tone; together they make a richer red than either one does alone. Let the other recipe of dough remain white (uncolored).

Cut out a thin cardboard rectangle, 3" × 4½", to use as a template.

Roll out the white dough to ¼" thick. Place the template on the dough and cut around it with a sharp knife; repeat to make as many dough rectangles as you can. Reknead the leftover dough, roll it out and cut out more rectangles. Set the rectangles aside on waxed paper. Repeat this process using red dough, to make an equal number of red rectangles. Stack the rectangles neatly, alternating the colors and brushing water between them to adhere them.

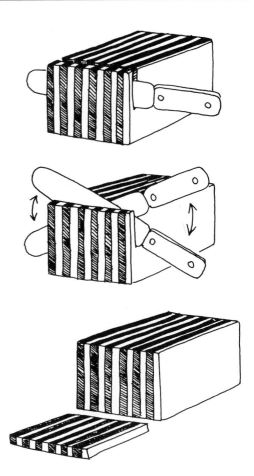

Turn the stack on its side. Using a sharp knife or long, narrow spatula, slice off a piece of dough about ¼" thick by first pushing the knife straight down and then rocking it back and forth gently until it cuts all the way to the bottom of the stack.

Cut two more slices, cleaning the knife between cuts.

2. Roll and cut the ornaments.

Dust the table with flour and place the slices in a row with the stripes running vertically as shown in the drawing. Leave 2" between the slices. Roll out the slices to ⅛" thick. **NOTE:** You will be rolling all three slices at the same time. Rolling

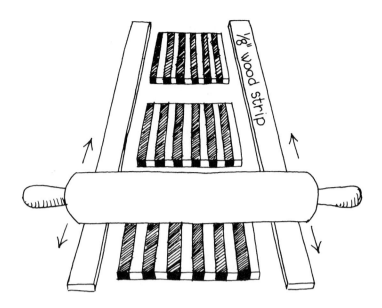

makes the slices the correct thickness and also presses the stripes together firmly.

Use the cookie cutters to cut out as many stars, trees, etc. as you can, dipping the cutter in flour before you press it into the dough. Try to use the surface area of the rolled-out dough efficiently, since you cannot reroll it. Use a plastic straw to make a hole in each ornament. Place the ornaments on waxed paper. Discard the leftover dough.

Cut three more slices from the stack of dough rectangles and repeat this process to make as many ornaments as you can.

After the ornaments have dried for two hours on one side, turn them over to dry for two more hours. Transfer them to wire racks to finish drying.

3. Add the cord or ribbon.
Fold the cord in half and push the loop up through the hole in the ornament. Slip the ends of the cord through the loop and pull them tight (Method #1, page 14). Tie to the tree, making a pretty bow.

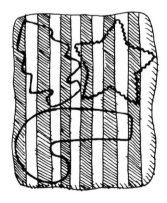

Flower Ornaments: Heart with Violets

Instructions are for making one ornament.

Photograph, page 58, for design and color guidance

1. Make the heart foundation piece.

Color some dough light pink. Roll it out to 1/8″ thick and cut a heart with the cookie cutter. Make two holes with a plastic straw, checking the drawing below for placement. Transfer the heart to waxed paper to dry, turning it often during the drying process so it dries evenly, without warping or cracking.

2. Make the violets and leaves.

Violets: Break off a bit of dough and color it lavender. (**NOTE:** Lavender is a combination of a little red plus a little blue color, mixed with white dough.) Roll it to 1/16″ thick and use the aspic cutter to make four violets. Use the blunt end of a wooden skewer to make three indentations in the center of each violet.

Leaves: Break off a bit of dough and color it green. Mold four or five little leaves and

use the back of a knife blade to make a center line in each.

Place the violets and leaves on waxed paper to dry.

3. Put the parts together.

When all the dough pieces are dry, glue them together with Sobo. First glue the violets to the heart, overlapping them slightly as shown in the drawing. Then glue the leaves in place around the violets. Let the glue dry.

4. Add the ribbon.

Tie one end of the ribbon through each hole in the ornament, making double knots (Method #8, page 14). Trim the ends of the ribbon on the diagonal.

MATERIALS

Cornstarch dough (page 25)

Paste food colors (red, blue, green)

Scalloped or plain heart cookie cutter, about 2¼″ wide

Flower-shaped aspic cutter

Sobo glue

Satin ribbon, 1/8″ wide, one piece 8″ long

59

Flower Ornaments: Basket of Flowers

MATERIALS

Cornstarch dough (page 25)

Paste food colors (blue, yellow, red, green)

Scalloped cookie cutter, 2½"-2¾" in diameter

Scalloped cookie cutter, 1¼" in diameter

Flower-shaped aspic cutter

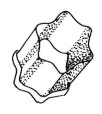

Sobo glue

Satin ribbon, ⅛" wide, one piece 18" long

Instructions are for making one ornament.

Photograph, page 58, for design and color guidance

1. Make the round foundation piece.
Color some dough light blue or work with uncolored (white) dough. Roll out the dough to ⅛" thick. Cut a round with the larger scalloped cookie cutter. Make a hole with a plastic straw. (See drawing on page 13.) Transfer the round to waxed paper to dry. Turn it often during the drying period so it dries evenly, without warping or cracking.

2. Make the basket, flowers and leaves.
Basket: Break off a bit of dough and color it yellow. Roll it out to a little less than ⅛" thick. Use the smaller scalloped cookie cutter to cut a round; cut the round in half to make two baskets. Set them aside on waxed paper to dry, turning several times during the drying period.

Flowers: Break off two bits of dough; color one light pink and another dark pink. Roll out each color to about ¹⁄₁₆" thick. Use the flower-shaped aspic cutter to cut three dark pink flowers and two light pink flowers. Color a bit of dough blue and roll tiny balls for the centers of the flowers. Place the flowers and centers on waxed paper to dry.

Leaves: Break off a bit of dough and color it green. Mold 6-8 tiny leaves and place them on waxed paper to dry.

3. Put the parts together.
When all the dough pieces are dry, glue them together with Sobo. First glue one of the baskets to the foundation. Then glue the flowers to the basket and to the foundation, checking the drawing on page 59 for placement. Let the glue dry.

Glue the blue centers to the flowers and glue the leaves around the flowers on the foundation and the basket. Let the glue dry.

NOTE: It's easiest to glue small pieces of dough by picking each one up with tweezers, dipping the back in glue and then placing it in position.

4. Add the ribbon.
Fold the ribbon in half. Slip the ends up through the hole in the ornament and tie them in a pretty bow on the front (Method #4, page 14). Trim the ends of the ribbon on the diagonal.

Flower Ornaments: Daisy Round

Instructions are for making one ornament.

Photograph, page 58, for design and color guidance

1. Make the round foundation piece.

Color some dough peach (a little red plus a little yellow coloring mixed with white dough). Roll out the dough to ⅛" thick and cut a round with the scalloped cookie cutter. Make a hole with a plastic straw. (See drawing on page 13.) Transfer the round to waxed paper to dry. Turn it often during the drying period so it dries evenly, without warping or cracking.

2. Make the petals, leaves and center of the daisy.

Petals: Break off a bit of dough and color it blue. Mold seven petals, each about ½" long.

Leaves: Color a bit of dough green. Mold three leaves and use the back of a knife blade to make a center line in each.

Center: Make a bit of yellow dough. Roll a ball about ¼" in diameter.

Place the petals, leaves and ball on waxed paper to dry.

3. Put the parts together.

When all the dough pieces are dry, glue them together with Sobo. First glue the ball to the middle of the scalloped round. Arrange the petals evenly around the center. Lift each petal with tweezers, apply glue to the back (or dip in a little puddle of glue) and replace in position. Glue the leaves between the petals, checking the drawing on page 59 for guidance. Let the glue dry thoroughly.

4. Add the ribbon.

Fold the ribbon in half and push the loop up through the hole in the ornament. Slip the ends of the ribbon through the loop and pull them tight (Method #1, page 14). Tie the ends to the tree with a pretty bow.

MATERIALS

Cornstarch dough (page 25)

Paste food colors (red, yellow, blue, green)

Scalloped cookie cutter, 2¼" in diameter

Sobo glue

Satin ribbon, ⅛" wide, one piece 18" long

White Heart

MATERIALS

Cornstarch dough (page 25)

Heart cookie cutter, 2½″ wide and 2½″ high

Sobo glue

Satin ribbon, ⅛″ wide, one piece 8″ long

The instructions are for making one ornament.

Photograph, below, for design and color guidance

1. Make the basic heart, holly leaves and berries.

Roll out some dough to ⅛″ thick. Cut a heart with the cookie cutter and use a plastic straw to make a hole in the heart. Transfer the heart to waxed paper to dry, turning it every couple of hours so it dries flat.

Roll 40-50 tiny berries and set them in a flat container to dry. Mold two tiny holly leaves (be sure the back is flat so it can be glued to the heart) and use a toothpick to make a center line in each. Let them dry on waxed paper.

2. Put the parts together.

When all the dough pieces are dry, glue the holly leaves and three berries in the center of the heart and a border of berries near the edge of the heart. Refer to the photograph for guidance. **NOTE:** Use a toothpick to put dots of glue right on the heart and tweezers to place each little berry and leaf in position. Let the glue dry.

3. Add the ribbon.

Slip one end of the ribbon through the hole in the heart and tie both ends in a double knot (Method #5, page 14).

Country Ornaments: Noel Redware Plate

These ornaments are made by molding dough over individual tartlet pans. Instructions are for making one ornament.

Photograph, page 64, for design and color guidance

1. Make the basic plate.

Put a little vegetable oil on a cotton ball and grease the wrong side of the tartlet pan. Put the tartlet pan on a cookie sheet, wrong side up.

Roll out some dough to a little less than ¼" thick and use the scalloped cookie cutter to cut a round. Center the round over the outside of the tartlet pan and check the fit; the overlap around the sides should be enough to accommodate two holes for the ribbon.

Make two marks, 1½" apart, to indicate exactly where you will put the holes. Remove the round of dough from the tartlet pan, lay it flat and make the two holes with a plastic straw.

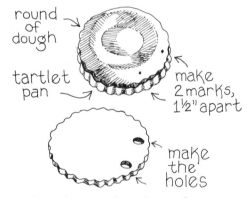

round
of
dough

tartlet
pan

make
2 marks,
1½" apart

make
the
holes

Replace the round on the tartlet pan, pressing the dough to conform to the fluted shape of the pan.

2. Bake the plates.

Bake at 250° for about half an hour or until the plate is hard enough to be removed from the tartlet pan without collapsing or losing shape. Turn the plate right side up and continue baking without the tartlet pan (so the inside bakes, too) until it is hard. Remove from the oven and allow to cool.

3. Paint and polyurethane the plate.

Paint with one coat of white. Let that coat dry and then give the plate two coats of terra-cotta-colored paint. When the terra cotta is dry, add "NOEL" in yellow and other decorations in yellow and green as shown in the drawing above. Let the paint dry thoroughly.

Brush on two or three coats of polyurethane, letting each coat dry before applying the next. Be careful not to clog the holes with polyurethane.

4. Add the ribbon.

Tie a knot near one end of the ribbon. Thread the unknotted end up through one hole and back down through the other; make a knot near that end, too (Method #9, page 14). Trim the ends on the diagonal.

MATERIALS

Flour/salt dough (page 16)

Tartlet pan with fluted edge, flat or partially flat bottom, shallow sides, 3" diameter (approximately) across top

Scalloped round cookie cutter, about 3¼" in diameter

Acrylic paints (white, burnt sienna or brown, yellow or yellow oxide, green); brushes

Polyurethane, brush, turpentine

Plaid taffeta ribbon, ⅜" wide, one piece 12" long

Country Ornaments: Christmas Cottage

The instructions are for making one cottage.

Photograph, page 64, for design and color guidance

1. Make the basic cottage.

Transfer the pattern to thin cardboard to make a template as explained on page 12.

Roll out some dough to ¼" thick. Place the template on the dough, hold it lightly and cut around it with a sharp knife. Following the dark lines on the pattern, make the lines in the roof using the back of a knife blade or the edge of a plastic ruler. Incise the lines clearly but be careful not to cut all the way through the dough. Carefully move the cottage to a cookie sheet or the back of a jelly roll pan.

2. Add the windows and door.

Roll out some dough to ¹⁄₁₆" thick. Cut out five rectangles, each about ⅜" high and ½" wide, for the windows, and one rectangle, 1" high and ⅝" wide, for the door. Following the dotted lines on the pattern for placement, brush water on the cottage and press each window and the door in position.

Use a plastic straw to make a hole in the top center of the cottage.

3. Bake the cottage.

Bake at 250° for half an hour and then run a spatula under the cottage to loosen it from the cookie sheet. Continue baking until the top is hard. Turn the cottage over and continue baking until it is completely hard. Remove from the oven and allow to cool.

4. Paint and polyurethane the cottage.

Paint with one coat of white, making sure you get paint into all the incised roof lines. Next, paint two coats of each color you see in the photograph on page 64. Start with the lightest and end with the darkest, letting each color dry before applying the next: Paint the cream-color (white plus a dab of brown) roof tiles on the top surface only, leaving the grooves between the tiles white; next, paint the yellow windows on the top surface only; paint red on the front, side edges and back; paint green on the remaining tiles and on the door, on the top surface only. Do any touch-ups that may be necessary.

When the paint is thoroughly dry, apply two or three coats of polyurethane, letting each coat dry before brushing on the next.

5. Add the ribbon.

Fold the gingham ribbon in half and push the loop up through the hole in the cottage. Slip the ends of the ribbon through the loop and pull them tight (Method #1, page 14). Tie to the tree, making a pretty bow.

MATERIALS

Flour/salt dough (page 16)

Acrylic paints (white, red, yellow, green, brown); brushes

Polyurethane, brush, turpentine

Gingham ribbon, ⅜" wide, one piece 20" long

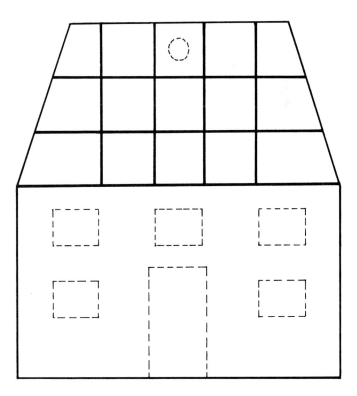

Country Ornaments: Christmas Baskets

MATERIALS

Flour/salt dough (page 16)

Light brown glaze (page 21)

Polyurethane, brush, turpentine

Gift wrap, one piece of red and one piece of green NOTE: The paper may have a small print, dot or check, if you like.

Sobo glue

Gingham ribbon, ⅜″ wide, one piece 20″ long for each basket

The instructions are for making several baskets at a time.

Photograph, page 64, for design and color guidance

1. Make the basic baskets.

Transfer the pattern to thin cardboard to make a template as explained on page 12.

Roll out some dough to ¼″ thick on the flour-dusted back of a jelly roll pan. Cut the dough into sections, each section large enough to accommodate the template. Place the template on one section of dough, hold it lightly and cut around it with a sharp knife, lifting away the excess dough as you cut. Repeat on all the sections of dough.

2. Bake the basic baskets.

Bake at 250° for about 20 minutes and then run a spatula under the baskets to loosen them from the jelly roll pan. Continue baking until the tops are hard. Turn the baskets over and continue baking until completely hard. Remove them from the oven and allow them to cool.

Brush the top sides of the baskets with light brown glaze and return to the oven

for about 15 minutes or until the glaze is set and dry. Remove them and let them cool.

3. Decorate and polyurethane the baskets.

Before applying the paper triangles, brush one coat of polyurethane on the baskets and let it dry thoroughly. While it is drying, cut the triangles out of gift wrap. For each ornament, cut out five ¾" squares—three red and two green OR three green and two red. Cut each square in half on the diagonal and discard one triangle; you need nine triangles per ornament.

Arrange the nine triangles on one basket, referring to the pattern for placement. Lift each triangle, apply glue to the back and replace it on the basket, smoothing it over the uneven contours of the dough. Wipe away any excess glue. Repeat this process for all the baskets. Let the glue dry thoroughly.

Brush on two more coats of polyurethane, letting each coat dry before applying the next.

4. Add the ribbon.

Slip the ribbon under the handle of the basket and tie the ends to the tree, making a pretty bow (Method #6, page 14). The basket should hang quite close to the branch of the tree.

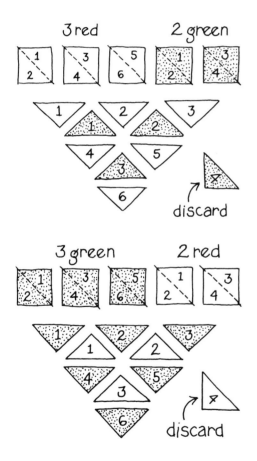

67

Country Ornaments: Farm Animals

MATERIALS

Flour/salt dough (page 16)

Animal cookie cutters, especially cow, horse, chick and pig

Paper clips (regular size), wire cutter

Acrylic paints (white, red, yellow or yellow oxide, burnt sienna); brushes

Polyurethane, brush, turpentine

Plaid taffeta ribbon, ⅜" wide, one piece 20" long for each animal

Photograph, page 64, for design and color guidance

1. Make the basic animals.

Roll out some dough to ¼" thick and use the cookie cutters to cut as many animals as you want. Transfer the animals to a cookie sheet. Make paper clip loops (see page 13 for more information) and insert a loop into each animal.

2. Bake the basic animals.

Bake at 250° for half an hour and then run a spatula under each animal to loosen it from the cookie sheet. Continue baking until the tops are hard. Turn the animals over and finish baking. Remove them from the oven and allow them to cool.

3. Paint and polyurethane the animals.

Paint one coat of white on each animal. When the white is dry, paint two coats of base color on each animal, referring to the photograph on page 64 for color guidance. Horses can be brick red, pigs might be dark terra cotta, chicks a butter yellow and cows an earthy gold. Let the paint dry thoroughly.

When that paint is dry, add the detailing: polka dots, hooves, tail and face on the horse; an outline and a face on the pig; spots, hooves, tail and face on the cow; feet, wing and face on the chick. Let the paint dry.

Brush on two or three coats of polyurethane, letting each coat dry before applying the next.

4. Add the ribbon.

For each animal, fold a 20"-long piece of ribbon in half and push the ribbon loop up through the paper clip loop. Slip the ends of the ribbon through the ribbon loop and pull them tight (Method #1, page 14). Tie to the tree with a pretty bow.

Gingerbread Folks Garland

Two recipes of bread/glue dough will yield about 80 miniature boys and girls.

Photograph, page 64, for design and color guidance

1. Make the basic boys and girls.

Color the dough gingerbread brown. Break off about one quarter of one recipe and roll it out to ⅛" thick. Try not to use too much flour when dusting the table and rolling pin. Use the miniature cookie cutters to cut as many little boys and girls as possible. Gather up the excess dough and rewrap it tightly.

Transfer the boys and girls to waxed paper. Make a hole in the top of each boy and girl by inserting a pencil point gently, first from the front and then from the back. The hole should be about ⅛" in diameter.

Incise the eyes and noses with the blunt end of a wooden skewer. Cut a small piece of plastic straw in half lengthwise and use the end (a half-circle) to incise the smiles. Use the blunt end of the wooden skewer to incise two buttons on each girl and three buttons on each boy.

Repeat this process with the remaining dough, to make as many gingerbread folks as you can. Let the boys and girls dry on the waxed paper for two hours; then turn them over and let them dry for two more hours. Transfer them to wire racks to finish drying.

2. Decorate the gingerbread folks.

Using the glitter pens, decorate the boys with dots of silver on the hands and dots of green on the feet. Decorate the girls with dots of gold on the hands and dots of red on the skirts. Let the glitter dry.

3. Join the gingerbread folks with crochet thread or string.

String the boys and girls on several short lengths of thread or string instead of trying to make one long garland.

Cut a five-foot piece of thread or string. Thread the end through the hole of one boy or girl and push the boy or girl to the middle of the thread. Tie a double knot. Working out from the middle, tie a boy or girl every three inches. Be sure they are all facing the same direction.

Repeat with several more lengths of thread until you have used up all the boys and girls.

MATERIALS

Bread/glue dough (page 22)

Paste food color (brown)

Miniature gingerbread girl cookie cutter

Miniature gingerbread boy cookie cutter

Glitter pens (red, green, silver, gold)

Red crochet thread or red string

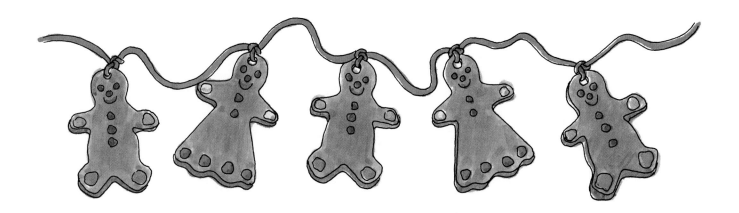

CHAPTER 3
THE TWELVE DAYS OF CHRISTMAS TREE

How many times at carolling parties and on Christmas Eve have you and your family and friends struggled to get those twelve gifts in the right order? The struggle usually ends in hilarity, but you'll never struggle again if your tree is decorated with this spectacular display of:

Twelve drummers drumming
Eleven pipers piping
Ten lords a-leaping
Nine ladies dancing
Eight maids a-milking
Seven swans a-swimming
Six geese a-laying
Five golden rings
Four calling birds
Three French hens
Two turtledoves
And a partridge in a pear tree.

GENERAL DIRECTIONS FOR MAKING THE TWELVE DAYS OF CHRISTMAS TREE

Making all 80 ornaments for the full tree is, without doubt, a major project—and a stunning one, as you can see from the photograph on page 70. The best approach is to do the work at a leisurely pace over an extended period of time. If you start in September (or even in July) and devote an occasional afternoon to making 12 or 15 ornaments, you'll be finished well ahead of the holiday rush. And if you can recruit some helpers, you'll be done even faster.

Do remember also that there are alternatives to making ornaments for the entire large tree: Make just one of each ornament to represent each of the 12 gifts; make several of each ornament you particularly like, not as part of any larger project but just because you like them; make just a few of each ornament (instead of the full complement) and hang them on a small tree.

Please note the following points:

■ Be sure to read the section on flour/salt dough, pages 16–21, before making any of these ornaments.

■ You will need several batches of flour/salt dough to make all 80 ornaments—perhaps as many as ten batches, depending on how economically you use the dough. Don't make all ten batches at one time; make two batches to start and additional ones as you need them.

■ The materials needed for each ornament are listed at the beginning of the instructions for each ornament.

■ Make at least one extra of each ornament; it would be a great pity if one ornament broke and the whole effect were ruined for lack of a replacement.

■ When you are making multiples of an ornament, make only four or five at a time. It is better not to have a lot of unbaked ornaments drying out while you make more and more. Bake all four or five at one time.

■ Remember to paint the back as well as the front of any ornament that requires painting.

Partridge in a Pear Tree

Photograph, page 74, for design and color guidance

1. Make the basic pear tree.

As you can see in the photograph on page 74, the pear tree has six pears. To make one pear, start with an oval of dough about 1″ wide, 1½″ high and ½″ thick. Shape it as shown in the drawing, making it narrower at the top and rounding the edges. The underside will be flat.

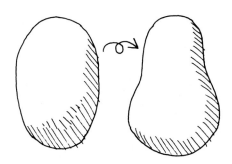

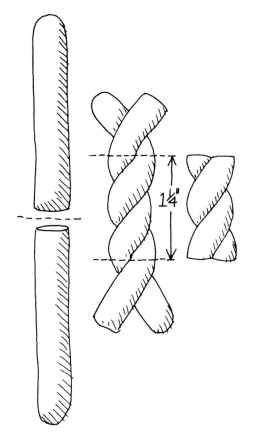

MATERIALS

Flour/salt dough (page 16)

Small bird cookie cutter

3 round wooden toothpicks

Acrylic paints (white, green, opaque gold); brushes

Polyurethane, brush, turpentine

Satin ribbon, ⅛″ wide, one piece 24″ long

527 cement

Make five more pears and place them on a cookie sheet. Arrange them in a pyramid and attach with a little water brushed between them. Press the pears together gently.

To make the trunk, roll a little dough into a rope about ¼″–⅜″ in diameter. Cut the rope in half and twist the two halves together. From this, cut a section about 1¼″ long and attach the section to the bottom center pear with a little water, pressing it gently so it adheres.

Make the stems: Break each toothpick in half and insert the pointed end of each half into the top of a pear, leaving about ½″ sticking out. Make the toothpicks point in slightly different directions.

2. Make the basic partridge and attach it to the pear tree.

Roll out a little dough to ¼″ thick. Use the small bird cookie cutter to cut out a partridge. If the bird seems a bit too small for the top of the tree, flatten it slightly to enlarge it. Mold a little wing for the bird (checking the photograph on page 74 for guidance) and attach the wing with water. Make the eye with the blunt end of a wooden skewer.

Place the partridge above the top pear on the cookie sheet, with a bit of water between the bird and the pear, and press them together gently.

3. Bake the partridge in a pear tree.

Bake at 250° for half an hour. Run a spatula under the ornament to loosen it from the cookie sheet. Continue baking, without turning, until the ornament is completely hard. Remove from the oven and let it cool.

4. Paint and polyurethane the partridge in a pear tree.

Paint the ornament with one coat of white. When the white paint is dry, paint the bird, the trunk and the stems with two coats of gold and the pears with two coats of bright green. Let each coat dry thoroughly.

Brush the ornament with two or three coats of polyurethane, allowing each coat to dry completely before applying the next one.

5. Cement the ribbon to the ornament.

Turn the partridge in a pear tree over. Use 527 cement to adhere the 24"-long piece of satin ribbon across the back of the top pear. Let the cement dry. Tie the ornament to a vertical branch at the top of the Christmas tree.

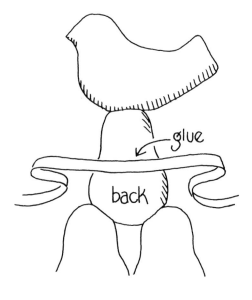

Two Turtledoves

Photograph, page 74, for design and color guidance

1. Make two basic turtledoves.

Transfer the turtledove pattern to thin cardboard to make a template as explained on page 12.

Roll out some dough to ¼″ thick. Place the template on the dough, hold it lightly and cut around it with a sharp knife. Pick up the template, turn it over and place it on another section of the dough so the bird is facing the opposite direction. Hold it lightly in place and cut around it. Carefully transfer the two turtledoves to a cookie sheet.

Use the aspic cutter to cut a heart in each dove, a plastic drinking straw to make the holes and the blunt end of a wooden skewer to make the eyes, checking the turtledove pattern for guidance.

2. Bake the turtledoves.

Bake at 250° for half an hour and then run a spatula under the doves to loosen them from the cookie sheet. Continue baking for another half hour and then transfer the doves to a wire rack. Continue baking until completely hard. Remove from the oven and allow to cool.

3. Paint and polyurethane the turtledoves.

Carefully paint the doves white. When the white is dry, paint two coats of silver, allowing the first coat to dry thoroughly before applying the second.

Brush on two or three coats of polyurethane, letting each coat dry before applying the next.

4. Add the ribbon.

For each dove, fold an 18″-long piece of ribbon in half and push the loop up through the round hole. Slip the ends of the ribbon through the loop and pull them tight (Method #1, page 14). Tie the ends of the ribbon to the tree, making a pretty bow.

MATERIALS

Flour/salt dough (page 16)

Heart-shaped aspic cutter

Acrylic paints (white, opaque silver); brush

Polyurethane, brush, turpentine

Satin ribbon, ⅛″ wide, one piece 18″ long for each dove

Three French Hens

MATERIALS

Flour/salt dough (page 16)

Acrylic paints (white, yellow, red, green, orange); brushes

Polyurethane, brush, turpentine

Satin ribbon, ⅛″ wide, one piece 8″ long for each hen

Photograph, page 74, for design and color guidance

1. Make three basic French hens.

Transfer the French hen pattern to thin cardboard to make a template as explained on page 12.

Roll out some dough to ¼″ thick. Place the template on the dough, hold it lightly and cut around it with a sharp knife. Repeat two more times to make three hens, turning the template over to make two hens facing one direction and one facing the other direction.

Place the three hens on a cookie sheet.

2. Add the details and wings to the hens.

Work on one hen at a time: Using a knife edge, incise the three lines of the beak. Make the eye with the blunt end of a wooden skewer. Roll three small balls of dough and attach them to the top of the head with a little water; flatten them slightly. Roll another small ball of dough and attach it under the beak with a little water; shape it like a teardrop. Use a narrow plastic straw or wooden skewer to make two holes in the body as shown on the pattern. The holes will close up a little during baking, so be sure to make them at least ⅛″ in diameter before baking.

Now make the wing, starting with the bottom row: Roll three little balls and shape each one into an oval. Brush water onto the wing area of the hen and place each ball in position as shown. Smudge the top edge of each oval to flatten and adhere it. Brush water along the smudged ends.

Make a second row of four ovals, over-lapping them on the first row as shown and smudging them as described. Brush water on the smudged ends. Make a third row of three ovals, overlapping them on the second row.

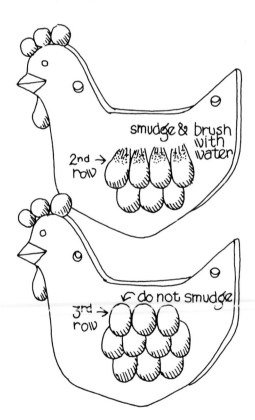

Repeat this process to make wings on the two remaining hens.

3. Bake the French hens.

Bake the hens at 250° for half an hour. Run a spatula under them to loosen them from the cookie sheet and then continue baking until the tops are hard. Turn them over, transfer them to a wire rack and bake until the bottoms are hard. Turn again and finish baking on the wire rack. Remove the hens from the oven and let them cool.

4. Paint and polyurethane the French hens.

Paint the hens white. When the white is dry, paint two coats of each color as shown in the photograph on page 74: Start with the yellow body, and then add the red, the green and finally the orange. Allow each coat and color to dry thoroughly before applying the next. Do any touching up that may be necessary.

When the paint is completely dry, brush on two or three coats of polyurethane, letting each coat dry before applying the next.

5. Add the ribbon.

For each hen, thread one end of an 8″-long piece of ribbon through one hole and tie a double knot. Thread the other end of the ribbon through the other hole and tie a double knot (Method #8, page 14). Trim off excess ribbon on the diagonal.

Four Calling Birds

MATERIALS

Flour/salt dough (page 16)

Acrylic paints (white, blue, yellow-orange); brush

Polyurethane, brush, turpentine

Satin ribbon, ⅛″ wide, one piece 12″ long for each bird

Photograph, page 79, for design and color guidance

1. Make four basic calling birds.
Transfer the bird pattern and the wing pattern to thin cardboard to make templates as explained on page 12.

Roll out some dough to ¼″ thick. Place the bird pattern on the dough, hold it lightly in place and cut around it with a sharp knife. Carefully transfer the bird to a cookie sheet. Slit the dough at the bird's neck as indicated by the dark line on the pattern. Bend the head around to overlap the body, brushing a little water into the overlap to secure the head in position.

Repeat this procedure three more times to make a total of four birds. **NOTE:** Make two of the birds facing one direction and two of them facing the opposite direction by simply turning the pattern over when you cut out two of the birds.

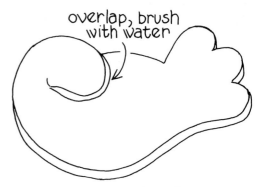

overlap, brush with water

2. Add the wings, beaks and eyes.
Roll out some dough to ⅛″ thick. Use the wing pattern to cut out four wings. Cut out four little triangles for the beaks.

Brush water on one bird and gently press a wing and a beak in position, checking the photograph on page 79 for guidance. Incise an eye with the blunt end of a wooden skewer. Repeat for the remaining birds.

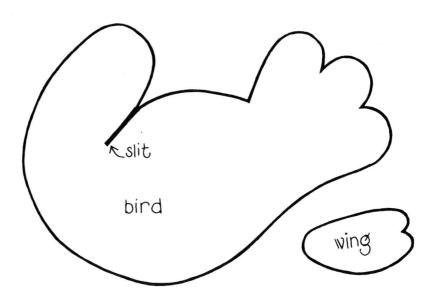

slit

bird

wing

3. Add thin rope outlines to the bird and wing.

To make the rope outlines you will need some moist, flexible dough; dry dough would crack or break when led around the curves of the bird and wing. If your dough is too stiff and dry, add a little water to moisten it.

Roll a very thin rope, about ⅛" in diameter and 12½" long. Brush water all around the edge of the bird. Place one end of the rope at the top of the bird and press gently. Continue pressing the rope in

place, following the shape of the bird carefully. End the rope outline under the head and cut off any excess rope.

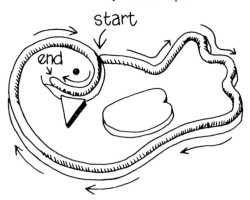

Roll another, shorter thin rope and follow the same procedure to outline the wing. Cut off any excess rope and join the ends neatly.

Use a wooden skewer or a narrow plastic straw to make holes at least ⅛″ in diameter, positioned as shown in the photograph on page 79.

4. Bake the calling birds.

Bake the birds at 250° for half an hour. Run a spatula under the birds to loosen them from the cookie sheet. Bake for another half hour, transfer to a wire rack and continue baking until the tops are hard. Turn the birds over on the wire rack and finish baking. Remove from the oven and allow to cool.

5. Paint and polyurethane the calling birds.

Paint the birds with three coats of white, letting each coat dry completely before applying the next one. Paint the rope outlines of the birds and wings with two coats of blue. Paint the beaks yellow-orange. Do any touch-ups that may be needed and let the paint dry thoroughly.

Brush on two or three coats of polyurethane, letting each coat dry before applying the next.

6. Add the ribbon.

For each bird, work with one piece of satin ribbon 12″ long. Tie a double knot near one end of the ribbon. Thread the un-knotted end through one hole from front to back and then through the other hole from back to front. Adjust the length so the apex is about 2½″ above the bird. Tie a double knot and trim off excess ribbon near the second knot (Method #9, page 14).

Five Gold Rings

Photograph, page 79, for design and color guidance

1. Make five basic rings.

Work with dough that is a little on the moist side; if your dough seems dry, knead in a few drops of water at a time to moisten.

To make one ring, roll two ropes each about 13″ long and about the thickness of a pencil. Move them to a cookie sheet and twist the ropes together as shown. Shape them into a ring about 3″ in diameter, cutting off any excess dough. Join the clean-cut ends together with a dab of water. Repeat to make a total of five rings.

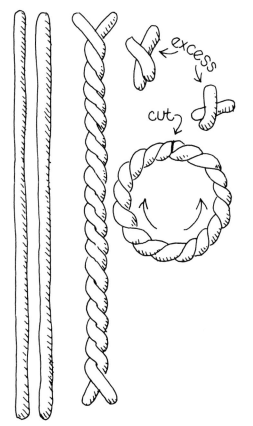

2. Bake the basic rings.

Bake the rings for half an hour at 250°. Run a spatula under the rings to loosen them from the cookie sheet. Continue baking, without turning, until they are hard. Remove the rings from the oven and allow them to cool.

3. Paint and polyurethane the rings.

Paint the rings with one coat of white. When the white is dry, paint two coats of gold, letting each coat dry completely before applying the next one.

Brush on two or three coats of polyurethane. Be sure to allow each coat to dry before applying the next coat.

4. Add the ribbon.

Tie a 20″-long piece of satin ribbon around each ring, over the joint. Make a double knot and then tie the free ends to the tree with a pretty bow.

MATERIALS

Flour/salt dough (page 16)

Acrylic paints (white, opaque gold); brush

Polyurethane, brush, turpentine

Satin ribbon, ⅛″ wide, one piece 20″ long for each ring

Six Geese A-Laying

Photograph, page 79, for design and color guidance

Instead of geese, here are silver eggs to represent the geese.

MATERIALS

Flour/salt dough (page 16)

Oval cookie cutter or round cookie cutter shaped into an oval, about 2″ wide and 2¾″ high

Acrylic paints (white, opaque silver); brush

Polyurethane, brush, turpentine

Wired berries, 2 units for each egg

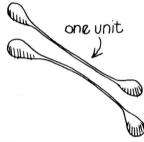

one unit

527 cement

Satin ribbon, ⅛″ wide: for each ornament, cut one piece 18″ long and 2 pieces each 7″ long

1. Make six basic eggs.

Roll out some dough to ¼″ thick. Using the cookie cutter, cut out six eggs and transfer them to a cookie sheet. Make holes at top and bottom with a plastic straw, checking the photograph on page 79 for guidance in placement.

Roll some dough into a short length of very thin rope (about ⅛″ in diameter). Cut off two pieces of the rope to fit across one egg, as shown in the photograph, and attach them with a little water.

Repeat for the remaining five eggs.

2. Bake the basic eggs.

Bake the eggs at 250° for half an hour and then run a spatula under them to loosen them from the cookie sheet. Continue baking until the tops are hard. Turn the eggs over onto a wire rack and bake until the bottoms are hard. Turn again and continue baking if necessary. Remove from the oven and allow to cool.

3. Paint and polyurethane the eggs.

Give the eggs one coat of white paint. When the white is dry, paint two coats of silver, letting each coat dry thoroughly.

Brush two or three coats of polyurethane on the eggs, letting each coat dry before applying the next.

4. Add the berries and ribbons.

Work on one egg at a time: Take two units of wired berries, fold in half and twist firmly together. Clip the wire short (but not so short that the berries come apart). Fan the berries out neatly and cement them to the egg.

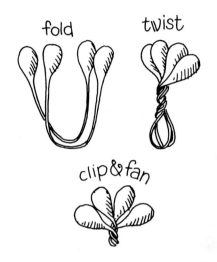

fold   twist

clip & fan

Fold two 7″-long pieces of satin ribbon together and push the ribbon loop up through the hole at the lower end of the egg. Slip the free ends of ribbon through the loop and pull tight. Do the same with one 18″-long ribbon, pushing the loop up through the hole at the upper end of the egg (Method #1, page 14).

Seven Swans A-Swimming

*Photograph, below, for design and
color guidance*

1. Make seven basic swans.

Transfer the swan and wing patterns to
thin cardboard to make templates as
explained on page 12.

Roll out some dough to ¼" thick. Place
the swan pattern on the dough, hold it
lightly and cut around it with a sharp knife.

With a spatula, carefully lift the swan and
put it on a cookie sheet.

Bend the neck as shown in the photograph and shape the end to form a beak.
Incise an eye with the blunt end of a
wooden skewer. Make two holes with a
narrow plastic straw or with the blunt end
of the skewer, as indicated on the pattern.

Make no more than four or five basic
swans before adding wings and baking the
swans as described in steps 2 and 3.
Repeat steps 1, 2 and 3 to make a total of
seven swans.

MATERIALS

Flour/salt dough (page 16)

Acrylic paint (white), brush

**Polyurethane, brush,
turpentine**

**Satin ribbon, ⅛" wide, one
piece 10" long for each swan**

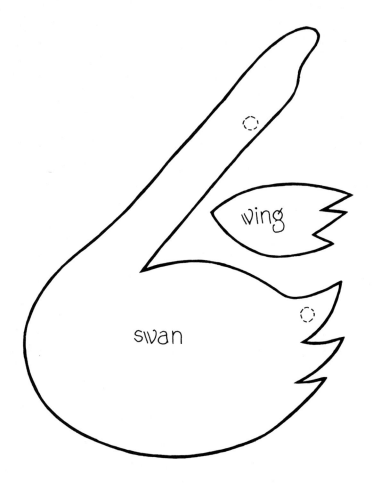

2. Add the wings.

Roll out some dough to ⅛" thick. Place the wing template on the dough and cut around it with a sharp knife. Repeat to make one wing for each swan. Brush each swan with water and press the wing gently in position on the swan, checking the photograph on page 83 for guidance in placement.

3. Bake the swans.

Bake at 250° for half an hour and then loosen the swans with a spatula. When the tops have hardened, transfer the swans to a wire rack, right side up. Continue baking, turning once, until completely hard. Remove from the oven and allow to cool.

4. Paint and polyurethane the swans.

Apply three coats of white paint to the swans, letting each coat dry before putting on the next. When the last coat is thoroughly dry, brush on two or three coats of polyurethane. Be sure each coat of polyurethane is dry before you apply the next.

5. Add the ribbons.

For each swan, slip one end of a 10" piece of ribbon through one hole and tie a double knot just above the swan. Slip the other end of the ribbon through the other hole, adjust the length of the ribbon and tie another double knot (Method #8, page 14). Trim off excess ribbon on the diagonal.

Eight Maids A-Milking

Instead of maids, here are milk pails to represent them.

Photograph, page 83, for design and color guidance

1. Make eight basic pails.

To make one pail, roll out some dough to ¼" thick. Cut out a rectangle 2½" wide and 2¼" high. Cut the sides of the rectangle at an angle as shown in the drawing. Transfer the pail to a cookie sheet.

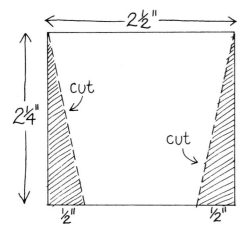

Make no more than four or five basic pails before decorating and baking as described in steps 2 and 3. Repeat steps 1, 2 and 3 to make a total of seven pails.

2. Add the decorations.

NOTE: When brushing water on the dough, brush *only* on the spots where decorations will be applied. Do *not* brush carelessly, because excess water may discolor the dough during baking.

Here's how to trim one pail: Roll out some dough to ⅛" thick. Using the aspic cutter, cut eight teardrops or four circles.

Cut them into half-circles and attach to the top and bottom edges of one pail with a little water, pressing gently in place.

Make a short length of very thin rope. Cut two pieces to go across the pail; attach them with water. Use a plastic straw to make two holes.

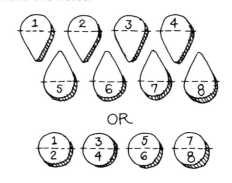

OR

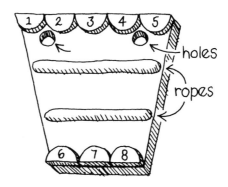

Repeat this process to decorate each pail.

3. Bake the pails.

Bake at 250° for half an hour and then run a spatula under the pails to loosen them from the cookie sheet. Continue baking

MATERIALS

Flour/salt dough (page 16)

Round or teardrop-shaped aspic cutter, ½" in diameter

Acrylic paints (white, blue); small, fine brushes

Polyurethane, brush, turpentine

Thin wire (flexible enough to bend easily, rigid enough to hold its shape when bent)

Wire cutter

until the tops are hard. Transfer to a wire rack and continue baking until completely hard, turning once. Remove from the oven and allow to cool.

4. Paint and polyurethane the pails.

Paint two coats of white on the *top surfaces only* of the half-circles and the thin ropes, letting each coat dry completely. Then paint over the white with two coats of blue. You must work carefully to keep from touching other parts of the pails with paint.

When the paint is dry, brush on two or three coats of polyurethane, letting each coat dry before applying the next.

5. Add the wire handles.

For each pail, cut a piece of wire 9″ long. Bend the wire in a U-shape as shown and slip each end through one hole of the pail. Twist each end back on itself, wrapping it around several times. Clip off excess wire with the wire cutter.

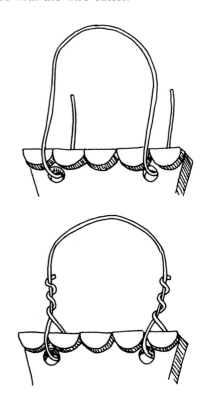

Nine Ladies Dancing

Photograph, page 83, for design and color guidance

1. Make nine basic ladies.

Work on one lady at a time. Roll out some dough to ¼″ thick and cut with the ginger-bread girl cookie cutter to make one lady. Transfer the lady to a cookie sheet.

Make her skirt wider by adding side panels: Cut a second lady and carefully cut panels from the skirt. Lift the panels and attach them to the first lady with a little water. Gather up the remaining piece of the second lady and knead it back into the main ball of dough.

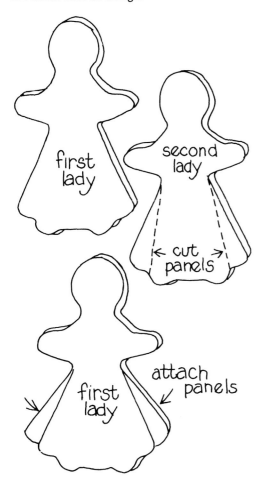

Make no more than four or five basic ladies before decorating and baking them, as described in steps 2 and 3. Repeat steps 1, 2 and 3 until you have made the nine dancing ladies.

2. Add the features and decorations.

NOTE: When brushing water on the dough, brush *only* on the spots where decorations will be applied. Do *not* brush carelessly, because excess water may discolor the dough during baking.

Work on one lady at a time: Incise the eyes, nose and mouth, using the blunt and pointed ends of a wooden skewer. To make the hair, press a small ball of dough through a garlic press until the strands are about ½″ long. Brush water around the top of the head. Use a toothpick to remove little bunches of strands and stick the bunches around the top of the head, poking them gently into position.

Roll four little balls of dough for the necklace. Dot water around the neckline and gently press the balls in place, checking the photograph on page 83 for guidance.

Use the back of a knife blade to incise four lines on the skirt. Be careful not to cut all the way through the dough.

MATERIALS

Flour/salt dough (page 16)

Gingerbread girl cookie cutter, about 5″ high

Garlic press

Flower-shaped aspic cutter

Acrylic paints (white, assorted colors); small, fine brushes

Polyurethane, brush, turpentine

Satin ribbon, ⅛″ wide: 2 pieces, each 10″ long, for each lady

527 cement

Make the skirt trims next. First make a thin rope of dough, ⅛″ in diameter and about 6″ long. Brush water on the skirt as shown and press the rope in place on the water, cutting off any excess rope.

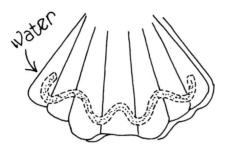

Now roll out some dough to less than ⅛″ thick and use the flower-shaped aspic cutter to cut out five flowers. Attach the flowers to the skirts and the feet with dots of water, following the photograph on page 83 for positioning. Use the blunt end of a wooden skewer to incise the center of each flower.

Mold about eight little leaves, attach them near the flowers with dots of water and make a center line in each leaf with the pointed end of a skewer or toothpick.

From the same rolled dough used for the flowers, cut a belt about ¼″ high and as wide as the lady's waistline. Attach with water and incise the little holes with the blunt end of a wooden skewer.

Repeat the decorating process on all the ladies you make.

3. Bake the dancing ladies.

Bake at 250° for half an hour and then run a spatula under all the ladies to loosen them from the cookie sheet. Continue baking until the tops are hard. Transfer the ladies to a wire rack and continue baking until completely hard, turning once. Remove from the oven and allow to cool.

4. Paint and polyurethane the dancing ladies.

Paint two coats of white on the *top surfaces only* of the necklaces, belts, flowers, leaves and rope trims. Let the first coat dry thoroughly before applying the second coat. Then paint two coats of each color shown in the photograph on page 83 or invent your own color scheme. Make a thin wash of paint plus water in an appropriate hair color (or several colors) and paint the hair. Work very carefully to avoid getting paint on the main body of each lady.

When the paint is dry, brush on two or three coats of polyurethane, letting each coat dry before applying the next.

5. Add the ribbons.

Cement two 10″ pieces of ribbon to the back of the head of each lady (Method #3, page 14). When the cement has set, tie each lady to the tree with a pretty bow.

Ten Lords A-Leaping

Photograph, page 90, for design and color guidance

1. Make ten basic lords.

Work on one lord at a time: Roll out some dough to ¼″ thick. Cut the dough with the gingerbread boy cookie cutter and transfer the lord to a cookie sheet. Immediately bend the arms and legs, as shown in the photograph on page 90. If you wait, the dough will begin to dry and will wrinkle unattractively when you move the arms and legs. Make the eyes, nose and mouth with the blunt and pointed ends of a wooden skewer.

Make one more basic lord and then proceed to step 2 to decorate the two lords. When you have made and decorated four or five lords, proceed to step 3 to bake them. Repeat this process until you have made all ten lords.

2. Add the decorations.

NOTE: When brushing water on the dough, brush *only* on the spots where decorations will be applied. Do *not* brush carelessly, because excess water may discolor the dough during baking.

Work on one lord at a time: Roll four small balls and attach them to the neckline with dots of water to make the collar. Roll six small balls and attach three to each boot with dots of water to make the boot trims, following the photograph on page 90 for positioning.

Roll three more small balls for the buttons, flatten each one and attach them with dots of water. Make a thin rope (about ⅛″ in diameter) and attach it to the waistline with water, cutting off any excess rope at each side of the waist.

To make the hair, force a little ball of dough through a garlic press until the strands are about ¼″ long. Brush water around the top of the lord's head. Using a toothpick or wooden skewer, lift a few strands at a time from the garlic press and transfer them to the head, poking them gently into position.

Repeat the decorating process on all the lords you make.

3. Bake the leaping lords.

Bake at 250° for half an hour and then run a spatula under the lords to loosen them from the cookie sheet. Continue baking until the tops are hard. Transfer the lords to a wire rack and continue baking until completely hard, turning once. Remove from the oven and allow to cool.

4. Paint and polyurethane the leaping lords.

Paint two coats of white on the *top surfaces only* of the collar, buttons, belts, boot trims and boots. Let the first coat dry thoroughly before applying the second coat. Then paint two coats of each color shown in the photograph on page 90 or invent your own color scheme. Make a thin wash of paint plus water in an appropriate hair color (or several colors) and paint the hair. Work carefully to avoid getting paint on the main body of each lord.

When the paint is dry, brush on two or three coats of polyurethane, letting each coat dry before applying the next.

5. Add the ribbons.

Cement two 10″-long pieces of ribbon to the back of the head of each lord (Method #3, page 14). When the cement has set, tie each lord to the tree with a pretty bow.

MATERIALS

Flour/salt dough (page 16)

Gingerbread boy cookie cutter, about 5″ high

Garlic press

Acrylic paints (white, assorted colors); small, fine brushes

Polyurethane, brush, turpentine

Satin ribbon, ⅛″ wide: 2 pieces, each 10″ long, for each lord

527 cement

Eleven Pipers Piping

MATERIALS

Flour/salt dough (page 16)

Acrylic paints (white, red, blue, green, yellow); brushes

Polyurethane, brush, turpentine

Satin ribbon, ⅛" wide, one piece 18" long for each pipe

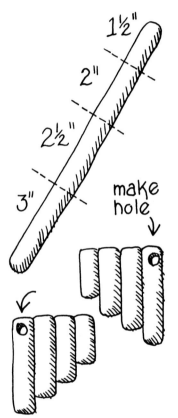

Instead of pipers, here are pipes to represent them.

Photograph, below, for design and color guidance

1. Make 11 basic pipes.

To make one pipe, begin by rolling a rope of dough about ½"–⅝" in diameter and about 9" long. Cut it into four pieces: 1½" long; 2" long; 2½" long and 3" long. Transfer the pieces to a cookie sheet and line them up in graduated order. Brush water between the pieces and press them together gently to adhere them to each other.

Use a plastic straw to make a hole in the longest piece.

Make four or five pipes at a time, placing some with the longest piece on the left and some with the longest piece on the right. Proceed to step 2 to bake the pipes. Repeat steps 1 and 2 to make a total of 11 pipes.

2. Bake the pipes.

Bake at 250° for half an hour and then run a spatula under the pipes to loosen them from the cookie sheet. Continue baking until the tops are hard. Turn over and transfer to a wire rack. Continue baking until completely hard, turning once more.

3. Paint and polyurethane the pipes.

Paint the pipes with two coats of white, letting the first coat dry thoroughly before applying the second. Then paint two coats of each color shown in the photograph below or invent your own color scheme. Don't forget to paint the ends and the backs. Work carefully when painting the colors, trying not to get red on the green and so on. Do any touching up that may be needed.

When the paint is completely dry, brush on two or three coats of polyurethane. Let each coat dry before applying the next.

4. Add the ribbon.

Thread an 18" piece of ribbon through the hole in each pipe and tie to the tree (Method #5, page 14).

Twelve Drummers Drumming

Instead of drummers, here are drums to represent them.

Photograph, page 90, for design and color guidance

1. Make 12 basic drums.

Transfer the diamond pattern to thin cardboard to make a template as explained on page 12. Keep the template handy, ready to be used as soon as step 1 is completed.

Work on the drums one at a time.

Roll out some dough to 1/8" thick and cut out a rectangle 2" high and 2 1/4" wide. Place it on a cookie sheet.

Roll out some dough to 1/4" thick and cut two strips of dough, each 2 1/2" wide and 1/4" high. Brush water on the cut edges of the rectangle at top and bottom, and butt a strip of dough, centered, against each edge.

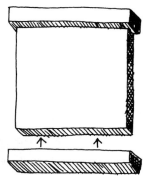

2. Add the diamonds.

Roll out some dough to 1/8" thick. Using the template, cut six diamonds. Cut two of the diamonds in half as shown.

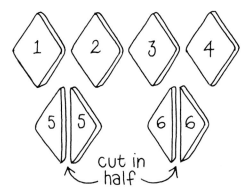

cut in half

Arrange the diamonds and half-diamonds on the drum, following the photograph on page 90 for placement. Attach by lifting each little piece, brushing water on the back of it (rather than on the drum) and then pressing it gently back in position on the drum.

Repeat this process (steps 1 and 2) to make the number of drums desired.

3. Bake the drums.

Bake at 250° for half an hour and then run a spatula under the drums to loosen them from the cookie sheet. Continue baking until the tops are hard. Turn the drums over onto a wire rack and finish baking.

4. Paint and polyurethane the drums.

Paint two coats of white on the *top surfaces only* of the upper and lower strips and all the diamonds and half-diamonds. Let each coat dry thoroughly and then paint two coats of the colors shown in the photograph on page 90 (or invent your own color scheme). Work carefully to avoid getting paint on the other parts of the drums.

When the paint is completely dry, brush on two or three coats of polyurethane. Let each coat dry before applying the next one.

5. Add the ribbons.

For each drum, fold an 8"-long piece of ribbon in half and cement the ends to the back of one corner (Method #2, page 14).

MATERIALS

Flour/salt dough (page 16)

Acrylic paints (white, red, green); brushes

Polyurethane, brush, turpentine

Satin ribbon, 1/8" wide, one piece 8" long for each drum

527 cement

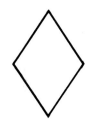

Wreaths are true signs of the holiday season. You see them most often on the front door, but they certainly don't have to go there. The five simple wreaths in this chapter, each with a very different look, can go just about anywhere in the house. Think about all the wonderful—even unexpected—places you can hang a wreath:

Over the mantel or resting right *on* the mantel

On a mirror in the entryway of your home

Around the newel post of a staircase

On the kitchen door

On an indoor windowsill   (See the photograph on page 105.)

Inside the back door

On a wall in the stairwell or stair landing

Over your desk

On a shelf of the breakfront

On the wall opposite your bed (or your child's bed), so you see it first thing in the morning and last thing at night

Holly and Berry Wreath

MATERIALS

2 recipes of bread/glue dough (page 22)

Paste food coloring (red, green)

Small, sharp scissors

Styrofoam wreath form, 12" in diameter, with Styrofoam about 1½" wide and 1¼" thick

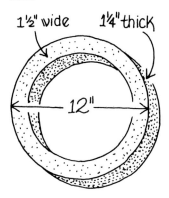

527 cement (or other clear cement made for use on Styrofoam)

Plaid taffeta ribbon, 1" wide, 2¼ yards for the bow

Sobo glue

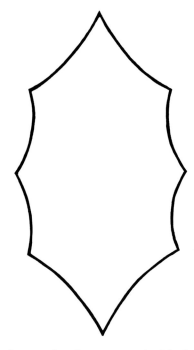

Photograph, page 92, for design and color guidance

1. Color the dough.

Color one recipe of dough a bright, deep green. Color two thirds of the second recipe of dough a lighter green. Color the remaining third bright red. (Check the photograph on page 92 for color guidance.) Wrap each color separately in plastic.

2. Make the holly leaves.

Transfer the holly leaf pattern to thin cardboard to make a template as explained on page 12.

Roll out half the deep green dough to ⅛" thick. (Rewrap the other half tightly in plastic.) Place the template on the dough and *outline* it with the point of a knife; do not cut through the dough. Outline the template as many times as possible, leaving about 1" between outlines.

Cut the outlined leaves apart with the knife. Now use small, sharp scissors to cut out each leaf on the outline. Make a center line on each leaf with the back of a knife, being careful not to cut all the way through the dough.

Gather up the leftover dough and knead it with the remaining deep green dough. Roll out the dough and make more leaves. Try to end up with about 30 deep green leaves.

Repeat this process with the light green dough to make about 24 more leaves.

NOTE: You will not need all the leaves you have made. Make extras so you can pick out the best-looking ones for your wreath. I used a total of 25 deep green leaves and 18 light ones.

Transfer all the leaves to waxed paper to dry for two hours on each side. If they have stiffened sufficiently after four hours, place the leaves on wire racks to finish drying. But if they are too floppy after four hours on the waxed paper, allow them to

dry for another hour on each side before moving them to the racks.

When the leaves are completely dry, brush one coat of polyurethane on each side, letting one side dry before turning them over to polyurethane the other side.

3. Make the red berries.

Using the red dough, roll 75 berries, each about ¼" in diameter. Transfer the berries to waxed paper to dry. Stir the berries around on the waxed paper occasionally so they dry evenly. Do not polyurethane the berries yet.

4. Cement the leaves to the wreath form.

The general technique is to use 527 cement to attach two leaves at a time to the wreath form, let the cement dry and then cement the next pair of leaves overlapping the previous pair. Place a small weight on the cemented ends of the leaves to hold them in position while the cement dries.

Start this way: Place a cotton swab across the wreath form. Apply a generous drop of 527 to one end of the *wrong side* of a leaf. Position the leaf at an angle, resting the uncemented end on the cotton swab. (The swab keeps the end of the leaf raised so that, when you have worked all the way around the wreath, the last leaf can be attached *under* the first leaf.) Now position a second leaf overlapping the first leaf at an angle. Observe where the second leaf touches the first leaf. Lift the second leaf and apply cement to the back, on all the spots where the two leaves touch and also at the end where the second leaf rests on the Styrofoam. Replace the second leaf in position, with a small weight on the cemented end to hold it in place while it dries. **NOTE:** I used small needle-nose pliers for the weight.

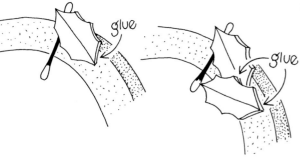

When the cement is dry enough to hold the two leaves in place, repeat the process with another pair of leaves. Be sure to apply cement wherever the leaves touch each other. Work all the way around the wreath form, checking the photograph on page 92 for guidance in the placement of leaves and the sequence of colors. When you have worked all the way around to the beginning, remove the cotton swab and then tuck and cement the last leaf under the first leaf. Let the cement dry thoroughly.

5. Cement the berries to the leaves.

Attach the berries to the leaves with 527 cement, following the photograph on page 92 for guidance. When the cement is dry, brush polyurethane on all the berries. Let the polyurethane dry.

6. Make and attach the bow.

Cut three pieces of taffeta ribbon, each 14" long, and three pieces, each 9½" long. Shape one piece into a loop and use Sobo to glue the ends together, overlapping them 1". Glue the loop together at the center as shown. Repeat with the other five pieces of ribbon.

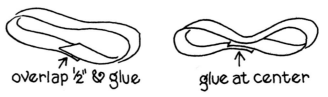

Glue the loops together in pairs (a short loop centered on a long loop) and then glue the three pairs together in a stack as shown, to make a bow.

Cut one piece of ribbon 3" long and another piece 5" long. Shape the 3" piece into a loop and glue the ends together, overlapping them ½". Do the same with the 5" piece. Glue the two loops together as shown, and then glue the pair of loops over the center of the bow. Let the glue dry.

Glue the completed bow to the wreath, checking the photograph on page 92 for correct placement.

Leaf and Berry Candleholder (medium size)

MATERIALS

Flour/salt dough (page 16)

Canapé cutter with straight sides, about 1½″ in diameter

Scalloped cookie cutter, about 2½″ in diameter

Acrylic paints (white, red, green, yellow oxide); brushes

Polyurethane, brush, turpentine

Each candleholder will accommodate a candle about 1¼″ in diameter. Use dripless candles so you won't have to clean off any melted wax. If some wax does drip on the candleholder, simply put it in the freezer for a few hours and then the wax will be easily removable.

Photograph, page 92, for design and color guidance

1. Make the foundation.

As you can see in the photograph on page 92, beneath the leaves of the candleholder is a foundation which supports the leaves and berries.

Apply a thin film of vegetable oil to the outside of the canapé cutter and place the cutter upside down on a cookie sheet. Roll a rope of dough ¾″ in diameter and 10″ long. Wrap it loosely around the canapé cutter and cut off the excess dough. Join the ends of the rope with water, neatly smoothing the joint. Leave the canapé cutter in place.

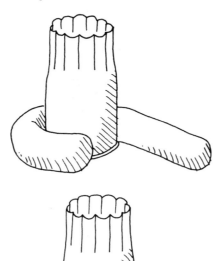

2. Make the leaves and attach them to the foundation.

Make no more than five leaves at a time.

Roll out some dough to ¼″ thick. Make each leaf with the scalloped cookie cutter, cutting out one side first and then moving the cutter over to cut the other side. The leaf should measure about 1¾″ from point to point. Use the back of a knife blade to make a deep indentation for the center line; be careful not to cut all the way through the dough.

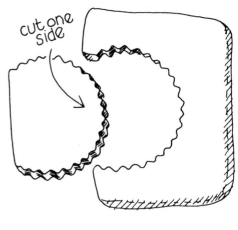

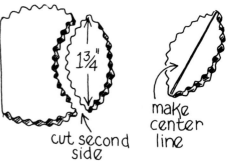

Brush water onto a 1″-wide section of the foundation. Place a leaf on the water, at an angle, with the tip of the leaf just short of the canapé cutter. Press gently to adhere. Now brush water on the left edge of the leaf and on another inch of the foundation. Place a second leaf overlapping the first leaf about ¼". Press gently to adhere it to the first leaf and to the foundation.

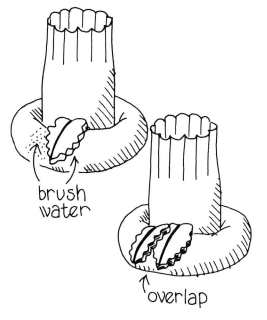

brush water

overlap

Continue in this manner, working all the way around the foundation. Tuck the left edge of the last leaf under the right edge of the first leaf.

3. Make the berries and attach them to the leaves.

Each berry is a ball of dough about ⅝" in diameter. Make a dozen berries; you may need one more or one less.

Brush water sparingly along the upper ends of the leaves. Place as many berries as needed to make a ring, brushing water sparingly between the berries, too. The last berry should close the ring. Make a shallow hole in each berry, using the pointed end of a paint brush.

make shallow holes

brush water between berries

4. Bake the candleholder.

Bake the candleholder at 250° for an hour and then run a spatula under it to loosen it from the cookie sheet. Continue baking until it seems to be done. Turn the heat off and leave the candleholder in the oven overnight. Remove from the oven. Take out the canapé cutter by pulling it down gently.

5. Paint and polyurethane the candleholder.

Paint the candleholder white, inside and out. When the white is dry, paint two coats of red on the berries (leaving the holes white), letting each coat dry thoroughly. Paint the sides and the center lines of the leaves medium green and let the paint dry. Brush the tops of the leaves with a lighter green. When the light green is dry, use a thin brush to paint medium green strokes on the right half of each leaf. (Check the photograph on page 92 for guidance.) Paint the foundation (including the bottom) with two coats of light brownish yellow. When all the paint is dry, go back and do any touching up that may be necessary.

Brush two or three coats of polyurethane on the candleholder, letting each coat dry completely before applying the next.

Christmas Stocking Wreath

MATERIALS

Flour/salt dough (page 16)

Round cookie cutter, about 2″ in diameter

Heart-shaped aspic cutter

Acrylic paints (white, red, green, blue); brushes

Polyurethane, brush, turpentine

Picot-edge satin ribbon, ³⁄₁₆″ wide, one piece 20″ long for each stocking

Real or artificial wreath about 24″ in diameter

Photograph, page 99, for design and color guidance

1. Make the basic stockings.

Transfer the stocking pattern to thin cardboard to make a template as explained on page 12.

Roll out some dough to ¼″ thick. Place the template on the dough, hold it lightly in place and cut around it with a sharp knife. Carefully transfer the stocking to a cookie sheet. Repeat to make nine stockings or as many as needed, turning some over to face the opposite direction. Leave two or three inches between stockings on the cookie sheet.

Using the 2″-diameter cookie cutter, cut a round of ⅛″-thick rolled dough and divide it in quarters. Brush the heel of one stocking with water and press a quarter-round of dough onto the heel. Cut out a little piece of rolled dough to fit the toe of the stocking as shown in the drawing. Brush the toe with water and press the toe piece in place. Repeat for all the stockings.

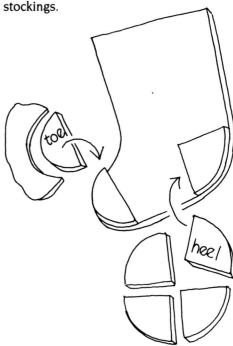

2. Trim each basic stocking with design #1, 2 or 3.

Follow these directions to trim every stocking with one of the designs shown in the drawings below and in the photograph on page 99.

Design #1: Make inch-wide "ribbing" by pressing the back of a knife into the dough (without cutting through the dough) to make a row of evenly spaced, indented lines. Use a plastic straw to make a hole in the corner above the heel.

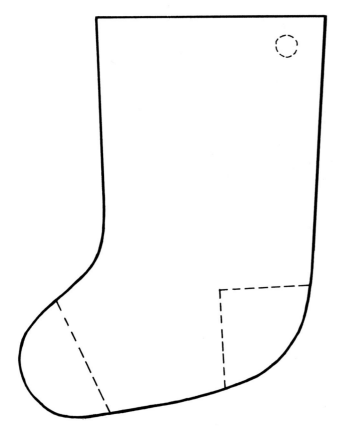

Roll out some dough to ⅛" thick and cut out two ½" squares. Brush water on the basic stocking and press the squares in place, checking the drawing below for guidance.

Design #2: Make the ribbing and hole as described above for Design #2. Roll out some dough to ⅛" thick and use the heart-shaped aspic cutter to cut two hearts. Brush water on the basic stocking and press the hearts in place, checking the drawing below for guidance.

Design #3: Cut off 1" of dough from the top of the stocking and discard it. Roll out some dough to ⅜" thick and cut a strip 1" high and slightly wider than the width of the stocking at the newly cut edge. Use water to butt the new strip of dough against the top edge of the stocking and press the two parts together gently.

Make the "ribbing" by firmly pressing the back of a knife into the attached strip of dough (without cutting through the dough) to form a row of evenly spaced, indented lines. Use a plastic straw to make a hole in the corner above the heel.

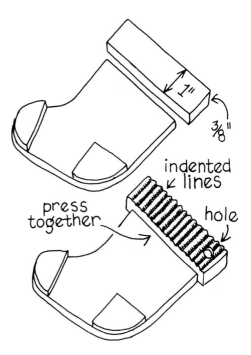

3. Bake the stockings.

Bake the stockings at 250° for about half an hour. Run a spatula under each stocking to loosen it from the cookie sheet. Continue baking, without turning, until the stockings are completely hard. Remove them from the oven and allow them to cool.

4. Paint and polyurethane the stockings.

Give the stockings one coat of white paint and let them dry. Carefully paint the stockings with two coats of the colors shown in the photograph (page 99) or paint them in your own color scheme. Let each coat dry thoroughly.

Brush each stocking with two or three coats of polyurethane, allowing the first coat to dry completely before applying the second.

5. Attach the stockings to the wreath.

Slip a 20" piece of ribbon through the hole of each stocking. Tie each stocking to a branch of the wreath and make a bow (Method #6, page 14). Be sure to arrange the stockings attractively, alternating the designs for variety.

Christmas Rose Wreaths

The instructions are for a pair of wreaths—one with red roses and white hearts and the other with white roses and red hearts.

Photograph, page 102, for design and color guidance

1. Color the dough.

Color one fourth of the dough bright green. Divide the remaining white dough in half: color one half bright red and leave the other half white. Wrap each part tightly in plastic.

2. Make six red roses and six white roses.

To make one red rose, start by pinching off a bit of red dough and rolling it into a ball about ⅜″ in diameter. Flatten the dough into an oval with very thin edges and roll it up from end to end to form the center of the rose. Flatten a second little ball of dough into an oval and brush water along the lower edge. Wrap it around the center of the rose, overlapping the center as shown, to make a petal. (The water acts as glue, adhering the petal to the center of the rose.) Repeat with a third oval, overlapping again.

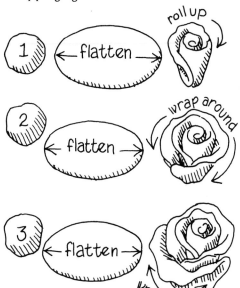

Add three more petals, making the flat ovals slightly larger. Attach with water, staggering the overlaps. To make the roses very realistic, bend the petals outward, pleat the lower edge of the last petal before attaching it to the previous petal, shape the last couple of petals in an undulating configuration and/or curl the very edge of one or two petals.

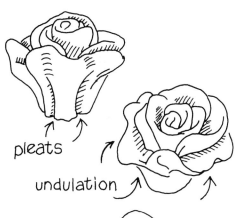

pleats

undulation

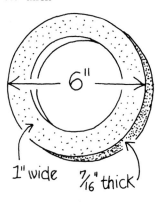

curled edges

Finally, carefully cut off the bottom of the rose with a sharp knife.

cut

Make five more red roses and then make six white roses. Place on waxed paper to dry. When the petals—but not the centers—are dry, transfer the roses to wire racks to finish drying all the way through.

MATERIALS

1 recipe of bread/glue dough (page 22)

Paste food colors (red, green)

Heart cookie cutter, about 1¾″ high and 1½″ wide

527 cement (or other clear cement made for use on Styrofoam)

2 Styrofoam wreath forms, each 6″ in diameter, with Styrofoam 1″ wide and about ⁷⁄₁₆″ thick

6″

1″ wide   ⁷⁄₁₆″ thick

3. Make 40–44 green leaves for the roses.

To make one leaf, take a little green dough and roll it into an oval about ¾″ long. Shape the ends to points and make a center line with the back of a knife blade. Repeat to make all 40–44 leaves. Let the leaves dry on waxed paper, turning them once or twice so they dry evenly on both sides.

4. Make and decorate six white hearts and six red hearts.

Make the white hearts first. Roll out some white dough to ⅛″ thick. Using the heart cookie cutter, cut out six hearts. Brush water lightly on the top side *only* of all the hearts so they won't dry out while you make the little leaf and berry decorations.

Leaves: Using a bit of green dough, make three little ovals, each ⅜″–½″ long. Flatten slightly and make center lines with the back of a knife.

Berries: Roll three tiny red balls.

Take one white heart and brush with a little more water. Lightly press the three leaves and three berries in place, checking the photograph on page 102 for guidance. Repeat this process on the five remaining white hearts. Then cut out six red hearts and decorate them in the same way, substituting *white* berries for red.

Place all 12 hearts on waxed paper to dry for a couple of hours. When they begin to harden, transfer them to wire racks to finish drying. Do not turn over.

5. Put the parts together on the Styrofoam bases.

When the roses, leaves and decorated hearts are completely dry, cement them to the Styrofoam wreath bases.

Make the red rose wreath first: Assemble the six red roses, 20–22 green leaves, six white hearts and one of the wreath bases. Mark the outer edge of the wreath base in sixths. Center a heart over each mark and cement in place. Let the cement dry.

Position the six roses between the hearts. Press each rose firmly into the Styrofoam to make an indentation. Lift each rose, put cement in the indentation and replace each rose exactly in position. Let the cement dry.

Cement leaves around the roses as shown in the photograph on page 102, tucking them under the rose petals. Let the cement dry completely.

Make the white rose wreath by the same method, using the remaining six white roses, 20–22 green leaves and six red hearts.

Hang the wreaths one above the other or side by side.

103

Merry Christmas Wreath

MATERIALS

Flour/salt dough (page 16)

Light brown glaze (page 21)

Red string or crochet thread for the loops

Real or artificial wreath, about 24″ in diameter

Photograph, page 105, for design and color guidance

1. Make, decorate and glaze the first letter.

Prepare the cookie sheet first: Draw several pairs of parallel lines 3¼″ apart. (Each letter will be about 3¼″ high; the parallel lines will be your guidelines.)

To make the first letter, an *M*, roll some dough into a rope about 15″ long and about ⅜″ in diameter. Put it on the cookie sheet and shape it to look like the *M* in the drawing below, positioning the *M* within the parallel lines. Cut off any excess rope and smooth the ends to make them neat.

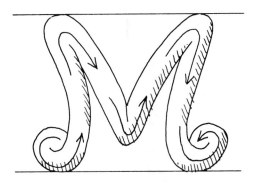

Decorate the letter using one of the five techniques illustrated below and shown in the photograph on page 105.

■ Make indentations with the end of a plastic straw.

■ Make indentations with the blunt end of a wooden skewer.

■ Poke little holes with the pointed end of a wooden skewer or toothpick.

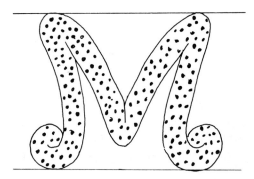

■ Make short lines with the back of a knife blade.

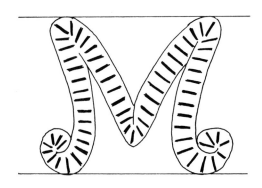

■ Make long lines with the back of a knife blade.

Now make holes in the top of the *M*, using a narrow plastic straw or the blunt end of a skewer. Check the drawing on page 106 for the position of the holes. Wiggle the straw or skewer around in the hole to enlarge it. The holes must be at least ⅛″ in diameter before baking because they will close up slightly during baking.

Brush the top and sides of the *M* with light brown glaze, taking care not to fill in the holes with glaze.

2. Make, decorate and glaze the rest of the letters.

Repeat Step 1 to make, decorate and glaze the remaining letters needed to spell out MERRY CHRISTMAS; you may wish to make extra letters in case any of the originals breaks or cracks. Follow the drawing below for guidance in shaping the letters and the photograph on page 105 for guidance in decorating the letters.

Fit as many letters as you can on one cookie sheet without crowding them too much. Draw parallel lines on a second cookie sheet and continue working on that.

3. Bake the letters.

Bake the letters at 250° for about half an hour. Run a spatula under each letter to loosen it from the cookie sheet. Continue baking until the letters are completely hard; do not turn them over during baking. Remove the letters from the oven and allow them to cool.

4. Polyurethane the letters.

Brush two coats of polyurethane on the letters, letting the first coat dry thoroughly before applying the second. Be very careful not to fill in the holes with polyurethane; they must remain clear so the string can be threaded through them.

5. Attach the letters to the wreath.

Cut and thread two 18″-long pieces of string or crochet thread through each and every hole. Lay the wreath down flat and arrange the letters correctly. (Check the photograph on page 105 for guidance.) Use the red strings to tie the letters to the branches of the wreath. Hang the wreath up and adjust the letters if necessary. Make pretty bows and trim off some of the excess string.

Straw Wreath with Glitter Trees and Gifts

Photograph, page 108, for design and color guidance

1. Make and bake the basic trees and gifts.

Roll out some dough to ¼" thick. Use the cookie cutter to cut out six trees (or seven, for a safety margin). Cut out six (or seven) gifts, each 1¾" square. Carefully move all the trees and gifts to a cookie sheet.

Bake at 250° until completely hard, turning once during baking. Remove from the oven and allow the pieces to cool.

2. Paint and polyurethane the trees and gifts.

Give all the pieces one coat of white paint. When that coat is dry, give the trees two coats of bright green paint and the gifts two coats of golden yellow. Let each coat dry thoroughly.

Brush on two coats of polyurethane, allowing the first coat to dry before applying the second.

3. Decorate the trees and gifts.

Decorate each tree with dots of gold and red glitter applied with glitter pens, as shown in the photograph on page 108. Let the glitter dry for several hours.

Decorate each gift first with two pieces of plaid taffeta ribbon, using Sobo to glue the pieces perpendicularly to each other across the front, sides and back. Let the

glue dry. Then glue on a small bow tied from a 10"-long piece of taffeta ribbon. Let the glue dry. Trim the ends of the ribbon on a steep diagonal.

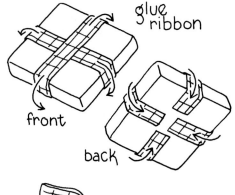

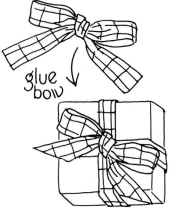

4. Glue the trees and gifts to the straw wreath.

Put the wreath down flat on a table. Arrange six trees and six gifts on it as shown in the photograph on page 108, spacing them evenly and allowing a clear area for the big bow.

Mix some epoxy glue. Lift each tree and each gift, apply epoxy to the back and replace on the wreath. Let the epoxy dry.

MATERIALS

Flour/salt dough (page 16)

Christmas tree cookie cutter, about 2" wide and 2¾" high

Acrylic paints (green, yellow); brushes

Polyurethane, brush, turpentine

Glitter pens (gold, red)

3 yards plaid taffeta (or other) ribbon, ⁵⁄₁₆" wide, for the gifts

5 yards dotted grosgrain ribbon, ⅞" wide, for the trim and bow

Sobo glue

Five-minute epoxy

Straight pins with glass-bead heads

Straw wreath, 14" in diameter

5. Attach the grosgrain ribbon between the trees and gifts.

Prop the wreath on a stack of books, with the back facing you. Wrap a piece of ⅞"-wide grosgrain ribbon around one section of the wreath, between one tree and one gift; the ends should overlap about ¾". Cut off any excess ribbon. Use Sobo to glue the ends together, and then secure them to the wreath by pushing a straight pin through both layers of ribbon, right into the straw. Repeat with ten more pieces of grosgrain ribbon, working around the wreath.

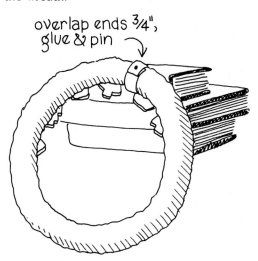

overlap ends ¾",
glue & pin

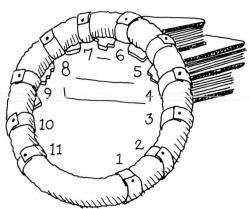

6. Make and attach the grosgrain ribbon bow.

To make the main part of the bow, cut three pieces of ⅞"-wide grosgrain ribbon, each 12" long. Shape each piece into a loop, overlapping the ends about 1". Use Sobo to glue the ends together and then to glue the loop together at the center. Stack the three loops as shown and glue them together. Cut a piece of ribbon 5" long and wrap it around the center, overlapping and gluing the ends on the back of the stack.

overlap 1" & glue

glue at center

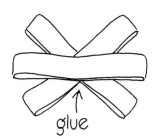

glue

wrap &
glue on the back

To make the tail of the bow, cut three 6"-long pieces of ribbon and two 7½"-long pieces of ribbon. Stack the pieces as shown and glue together at the top. Cut the opposite ends in points.

Before gluing the bow to the tail, first test for correct positioning by holding the bow and tail against the wreath, fitting them into the clear space allowed for the bow. Then glue the completed bow in place on the wreath with epoxy.

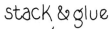

stack & glue

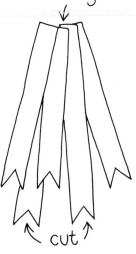

cut

Thischapter includes all kinds of delightful things for enhancing a holiday dinner table, buffet table or sideboard.

Children will love making and eating the cookie projects—especially the Cookie Train and the Little Gingerbread House Favors. They'll enjoy seeing their names on the Jolly Reindeer Place Markers, too.

Grown-ups will take pleasure in making and using Leaf and Berry Candleholders or the endearing Nativity Scene. And for grown-up eating, try your hand at a party dessert—a beautiful stacked Cookie Tree or a sophisticated Gingerbread Christmas Tree decorated with hearts, birds and stars.

Of course, the cookies and gingerbread will disappear quickly, but the candleholders and other permanent projects can be stored carefully in lots of tissue paper and used year after year—the start of a family tradition.

Little Gingerbread House Favors

MATERIALS

1 recipe of gingerbread dough (page 27)
NOTE: One recipe of dough should make about three little houses.

1 recipe of decorator icing (page 29)

1 decorating bag

#5, #7 and #27 icing tips, one of each

Assorted small candies: imperials (little round candies); cinnamon red-hots; gumdrops; licorice drops

Foil-wrapped chocolate Santa

The instructions are for making one little house; make one for each child at your holiday table.

Photograph, page 110, for design and color guidance

1. Make and bake the basic parts of the house.

Although the instructions are for making one house, you may, of course, make the parts for several houses at one time by cutting out several of each part whenever you roll out the dough.

Transfer the patterns to thin cardboard to make templates as explained on page 12. For each little house you must cut out one gingerbread base, two gingerbread sides (Side A and Side B), two gingerbread roof pieces (Roof A and Roof B), plus a gingerbread front and a gingerbread back.

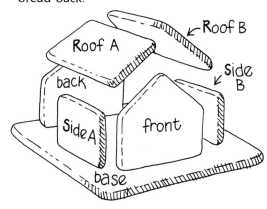

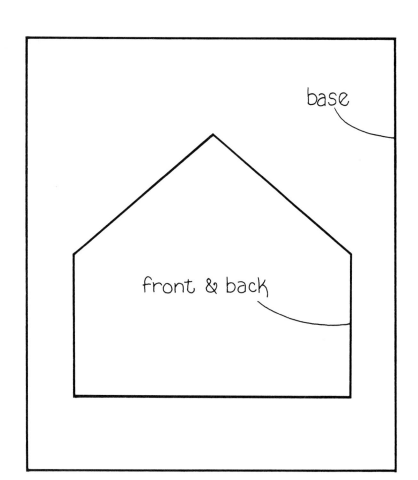

base

front & back

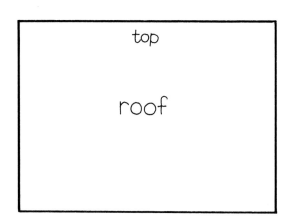

top

roof

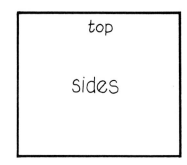

top

sides

112

On the flour-dusted back of a jelly roll pan, roll out half a recipe of dough at a time to ¼" thick. Place each template on the dough, hold lightly and cut around it with a sharp knife. Be sure to leave 1½" between the parts, since the dough spreads during baking. Lift away the excess dough as you cut, gather it together and knead it to make a smooth ball of dough; refrigerate the dough until it is needed for rerolling to make more parts of the houses.

NOTE: Be generous in sprinkling flour on the dough, jelly roll pan and rolling pin during the rolling process; this is a sticky dough. If the rolled-out dough becomes too soft and difficult to cut, return it to the refrigerator to firm up for a few minutes. Wipe the sharp knife often and dip it in flour when you cut the parts.

Bake the parts for ten minutes, according to the recipe. For this project it is better to overbake the cookies by a minute or two than to underbake them; they should be quite firm when you assemble them to make the house. When the cookies are cool, wipe off any excess flour with a damp paper towel.

2. Assemble the parts with icing.

Put the #7 icing tip on the decorating bag and fill the bag with white icing. Work on a piece of waxed paper.

Arrange the front, back and two sides on the base, holding them lightly in place to get an idea of how to center them.

Begin by attaching the back to the base: Pipe a generous line of icing on the bottom edge and just inside one side edge.

Press the back in place on the base and immediately pipe another line of icing on the base as shown. Add Side A, pressing it firmly against the base and the back.

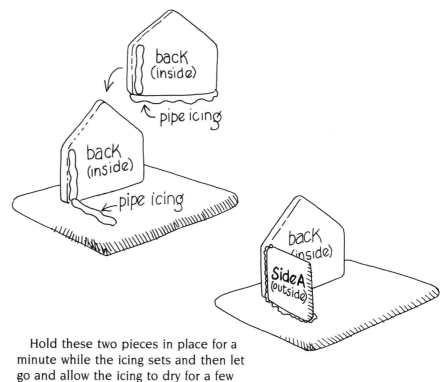

Hold these two pieces in place for a minute while the icing sets and then let go and allow the icing to dry for a few minutes.

Now take Side B and pipe a line of icing on the bottom edge and on the side edge as shown. Press Side B firmly in place against the back and the base. Let the icing dry for a few minutes.

Attach the front: Pipe a line of icing on the bottom edge and a line just inside each side edge as shown. Press the front firmly in place against the base and sides A and B. Let the icing dry for a few minutes.

3. Pipe the first group of decorations with the #27 icing tip.

Remove the #7 icing tip from the decorating bag and replace it with the #27 tip. Practice making little flowers on a piece of waxed paper.

Pipe a row of flowers at each corner of the house to conceal the joints at the front, back and sides.

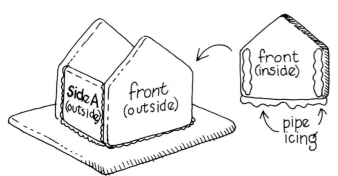

Pipe icing along one slanted edge each of the front and back and along the top edge of Side A as shown. Press Roof A firmly in place against the icing. Let the icing dry for a few minutes.

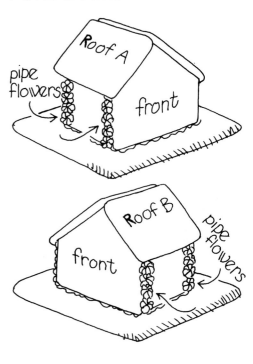

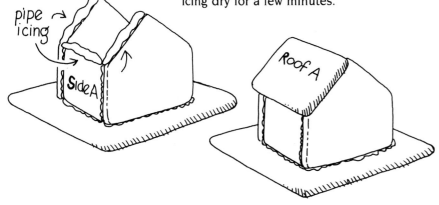

Pipe icing along the four remaining edges and press Roof B firmly in place against the icing. Let all the icing dry for half an hour.

Cut two gumdrops as shown, and put them together with a bit of icing to make a chimney.

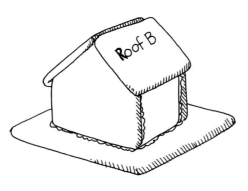

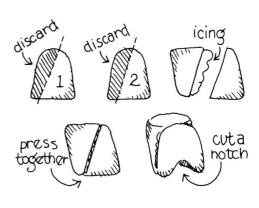

Pipe a small mound of icing on the roof and press the chimney in place. Let the icing dry for a few minutes.

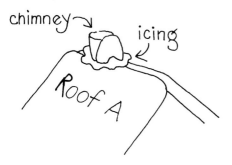

Now pipe a row of flowers all around the edge of Roof A, across the top and around the chimney. Repeat on the opposite side (Roof B). Let the icing dry for a few minutes.

4. Attach the candy decorations.

Each candy is attached by piping icing onto the house and pressing the candy in place on the icing; take another look at the photograph on page 110 to see the placement of the candies. Remove the #27 icing tip from the decorating bag and replace it with the #5 icing tip.

Front of the house: To make the door, which should be placed slightly off-center, begin by piping a short line of icing at the joint of the front and the base. Press a licorice drop in place on the icing. Pipe another line of icing on the first licorice drop and press a second drop in place. Continue in this fashion until five drops are stacked up to make the door.

Pipe dots of icing around the door, pressing an imperial onto each dot. Pipe a dot of icing, centered, on the front of the house and press half a gumdrop or an imperial onto the dot to make the upper window. Pipe a squiggle of icing in front of the door and press three imperials onto it to make the path.

Pipe icing on the back of a chocolate Santa and press him in place next to the door, with his feet on the base.

Sides of the house: Pipe three mounds of icing on the base on Side A; press a gumdrop or licorice candy on each mound to make the shrubs. Repeat on Side B.

Roof of the house: Pipe five dots in a row near the top of Roof A and press a cinnamon red-hot onto each dot. Now pipe three dots down in a row as shown and press a red-hot onto each dot.

Pipe the rest of the dots needed to fill out the roof and press a red-hot onto each dot. Repeat on Roof B.

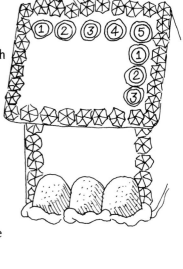

5. Add the icing snowdrift around the house.

Using the white icing and the #5 tip, pipe "snow" all around the house, moving the tip in a wavy pattern. The icing should extend almost to the edge of the base. Be sure to fill in the spaces around the shrubs, Santa and path. Let the icing dry overnight.

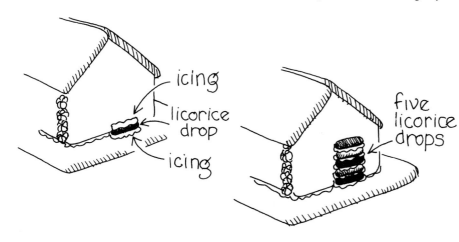

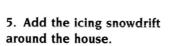

Jolly Reindeer Place Marker

MATERIALS

1–2 recipes of cookie dough (page 27)
NOTE: If you are making more than ten place markers, you will need a third recipe of dough.

Reindeer cookie cutter

1 recipe of decorator icing (page 29)

Paste food colors (red, green)

3 decorating bags

2 #2 icing tips

1 #7 icing tip

Each place marker is made up of two reindeer cookies on a cookie base.

Photograph, page 110, for design and color guidance

1. Make and bake the basic reindeer.

For each place marker you will need two reindeer, one facing left and one facing right.

On a floured surface, roll out half a recipe of dough at a time to about ¼" thick. Using the cookie cutter, cut as many reindeer as you need. Lift away the excess dough and gather it into a ball for rerolling. Transfer all the reindeer to a cookie sheet, turning half the reindeer over to face the opposite direction. Leave 1½" between reindeer. Manipulate the dough to straighten out each leg as shown in the drawing.

Bake the cookies according to the recipe.

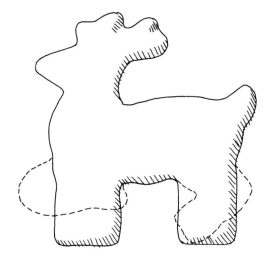

2. Make and bake the cookie bases.

For each place marker you will need a rectangular cookie base on which to stand a pair of reindeer.

Roll out some dough to ¼" thick. Cut as many rectangles, each 4½" × 3", as you need. Transfer them to the cookie sheet and bake according to the recipe.

3. Decorate the reindeer.

Place about half a cup of white icing in a small bowl and color it red. Put a #2 icing tip on one of the decorating bags and fill the bag with red icing. Place about half a cup of white icing in another small bowl and color it green. Put a #2 icing tip on another decorating bag and fill it with green icing. Put the #7 icing tip on the third decorating bag and fill the bag with white icing.

Line up all the reindeer that face right; set aside the remaining reindeer for now. With the red icing, pipe a smile and a name on each reindeer. With the green icing, pipe the eyes, the outlines and the dots on the letters. Let the icing dry.

4. Assemble the place markers.

First match up the reindeer in pairs—one facing right (with piped name) and one facing left (no piping) for each pair.

Here's how to assemble one place marker: With a small spatula, spread icing on a cookie base, to form a rectangle 2" × 3¼" and ¼" thick. Place a pair of reindeer on the cookie base, wrong sides on the inside, and facing in the same direction, with their feet in the icing about 1" apart. Press the feet firmly into the icing, all the way down to the cookie base. Hold both reindeer with one hand and, using the #7 tip, pipe white icing along the inside top edge of the antlers. Let the reindeer tilt toward each other and touch at the antlers; the icing will make them stick together. Let the icing dry.

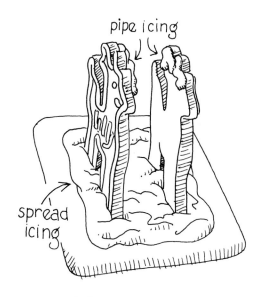

pipe icing

spread icing

Pipe a little more icing around the feet to secure them even better. When that icing dries, pipe another layer of icing all over the existing icing, working in a wavy motion; check the photograph on page 110 for guidance. Be sure to extend the icing out a little farther around the base, leaving about a ¼" border of cookie on all four sides. Finally, pipe a little white icing on the nose, antler and back of each reindeer. Let the icing dry overnight.

Repeat this process to make the rest of the place markers.

Cookie Forest Centerpiece

MATERIALS

1 recipe of cookie dough (page 27)

Large Christmas tree cookie cutter, about 4″ high

Small Christmas tree cookie cutter, about 3¼″ high

1 cup sugar, ½ cup water

Pastry brush

Green crystal sugar

1 recipe of decorator icing (page 29)

1 decorating bag

#5 and #7 tips, one of each

Flat base (as described in introduction)

3-4 ounces of shredded coconut (half of a 7-ounce bag)

Make the trees first and then assemble the forest on a flat base. For the photograph on page 110 I used a translucent green glass serving dish that has a center divider; you might like a round, white china plate, an oval ironstone platter, a carved wood tray or an enamelled spatterware dish. Any style is suitable as long as the piece you choose has a flattish bottom.

Photograph, page 110, for design and color guidance

1. Make and bake the basic tree cookies.

Each complete tree is composed of one *whole* baked tree cookie plus two baked *halves* of a tree cookie, the three parts attached with white icing. The number of complete trees you will need for your centerpiece depends on the size of the plate, serving dish or tray you are using for the base. I used four large trees and four small trees. No matter how many you decide you actually need, make three additional complete trees of each size.

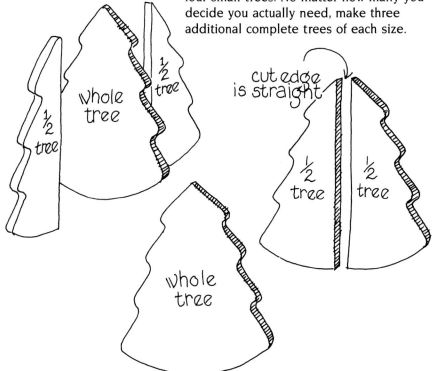

Any leftover dough can be cut with the cookie cutters to make extra cookies for munching.

Roll out half the dough at a time on a floured surface, to a little less than ¼″ thick. First cut as many *whole* large and small tree cookies as you need, plus three extra of each. Transfer to a cookie sheet, leaving 1″ between cookies. Now cut out the same number of tree cookies again, cut each one in half and transfer the halves to a cookie sheet. Be sure the cut edge is straight when you place each half on the cookie sheet.

Bake and cool the cookies according to the recipe. For this project it is preferable to overbake the cookies by a minute or two than to underbake them; browner cookies are stronger and stand up better when assembled to make the trees.

2. Decorate the tree cookies with crystal sugar.

Heat the sugar and water together in a small saucepan until the sugar melts, to make a thin syrup. Using a pastry brush, paint syrup on the front of one whole-tree cookie and sprinkle immediately with green crystal sugar. Set aside on waxed paper to dry. Repeat with all the whole trees and half-trees.

When the syrup is dry, turn the cookies over and repeat this process on the backs of the tree cookies. When the backs are dry, tap each cookie lightly to shake off any excess sugar.

Do *not* brush syrup on the edges of the tree cookies.

3. Decorate the edges of the tree cookies with shredded coconut.

Pour the coconut out in a mound on a piece of waxed paper or a small bowl. Attach the #5 icing tip and fill the decorating bag with white icing. Pipe a line of icing on one notched edge of one tree cookie. Press the edge firmly into the coconut. Repeat on the other side of the tree and on all the other whole-tree and half-tree cookies. Do *not* decorate the straight edges of any of the halves. Set aside on waxed paper to dry.

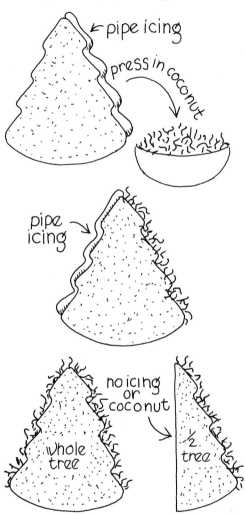

4. Put the cookies together to make trees.

Here's how to make one tree: Set out one large whole-tree cookie and two large half-tree cookies. Pipe a line of icing on the straight edge of one of the halves. Center it and press it firmly in place against the whole-tree cookie as shown. Hold it for

a few seconds and then allow it to stand and set for a few minutes. Repeat with the second half on the other side of the whole-tree cookie.

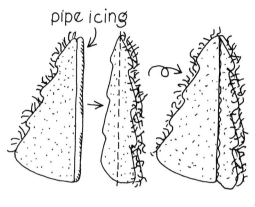

When the icing has hardened somewhat, carefully move the three-dimensional tree aside to dry thoroughly.

Repeat this process to make all the large and small trees.

5. Assemble the centerpiece.

Place the trees on the flat base in an arrangement that pleases you. Note the arrangement and then remove the trees. With a small spatula, spread a ½″-thick layer of icing on the base in the area where the trees will be placed; do not spread the icing all the way to the edges of the plate or tray. Immediately replace the trees in position, pressing them firmly into the icing until they touch the base underneath. Let the icing dry for a few minutes.

Change to the #7 icing tip. Pipe more icing around the trunks of the trees and let the icing dry for a few minutes. Now pipe another complete layer of icing all over the previous layer, sprinkling coconut on the wet icing as you go; work in small sections, one section at a time. Let the icing dry overnight.

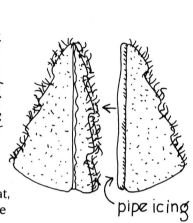

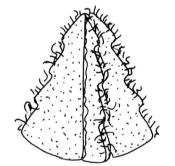

Nativity Scene

MATERIALS

Bread/glue dough (page 22)

Paste food colors (red, blue, green, brown, yellow)

Cookie cutters: scalloped round, about 2¼" in diameter; sheep; lamb; horse; cow; goat; dog; star, about 1½" wide

Fluted pastry cutter

Garlic press

Foamcore, one piece 20" high and 30" wide

Mat knife or single-edge razor blade

Sobo glue

Acrylic paints (blue, white); wide brush

Satin ribbon, 1" wide, 2 pieces each 7" long

Packing straw

Tweezers

This is an elaborate project with many parts to make, but no single part is particularly difficult to do. The people and animals are fashioned separately and set aside to dry while you make the foamcore background; when all the parts are dry and ready (it may take several days), glue them together to make the completed scene.

Photograph, page 121, for design and color guidance

NOTE: Color the dough in small amounts, as you need it, making a little more of each color than you think you need so you don't run out of it inconveniently. Wrap each color tightly in plastic.

1. Make the infant figure.

You will need a little piece of light blue dough and a little piece of skin-color dough.

To make the blanket, roll out the light blue dough to ⅛" thick and use the scalloped cookie cutter to cut a round. Set the round aside while you make the infant: Shape some skin-color dough into an oval about 1¾" long and ½" in diameter; shape one end into a head and neck, adding rough features if you like.

Center the baby on the light blue round, adhere it with a dab or two of water underneath and fold the round up over the baby. Brush water in the overlap so the blanket stays in place. Flare out the blanket around the infant's head as shown in the drawing. Place on waxed paper to dry.

2. Make the Mary figure.

You will need a piece of red dough, a little piece of skin-color dough, a tiny piece of light green dough and a piece of uncolored dough.

Work on waxed paper.

With red dough, mold a flat, bell-shape dress about 2½"–2¾" high, 2¼" wide and ⅛"–¼" thick. Flatten the top slightly to prepare it for the head.

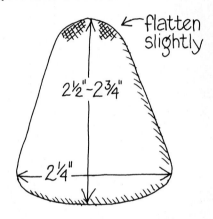

To make the head, roll a small ball of skin-color dough and flatten it to make a round, about 1" in diameter. Brush water across the top of the dress and press the head into position, overlapping it on the dress slightly. To make the hand, roll a small oval of skin-color dough, flatten it a little at one end and tuck it under the body with a dab of water. Do the same thing with a bit of light green dough to make the shoe.

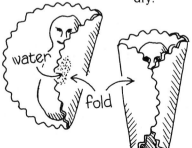

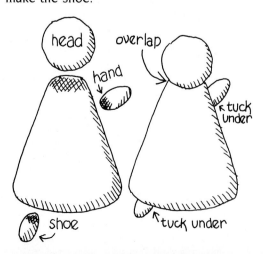

To make the scarf, flatten a piece of uncolored dough and shape it as shown in the drawing. Make sure the scarf curves around and covers the head and back. Trim off the edges with a fluted pastry cutter. Brush water on the back of the scarf and press it into position on the head and dress. Decorate the scarf with tiny balls of red dough attached with dots of water.

Leave the figure on the waxed paper either until the top seems dry or until the figure begins to curl; transfer it carefully, on a spatula, to a wire rack to finish drying.

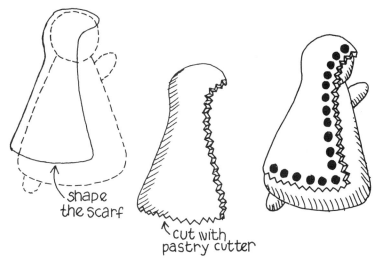

shape the scarf

cut with pastry cutter

3. Make the Joseph figure.

You will need a piece of light green dough, a little piece of skin-color dough and a piece of uncolored dough.

Work on waxed paper.

With light green dough, shape a flat robe about 4″ high, 2½″ wide and ⅛″–¼″ thick. Flatten the top slightly to prepare it for the head.

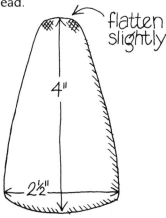

To make the head, roll a small ball of skin-color dough and flatten it to make a round, about 1″ in diameter. Brush water across the top of the robe and press the head into position, overlapping the robe slightly. To make the hand, roll a small oval of skin-color dough, flatten it a little at one end and tuck it under the body with a dab of water.

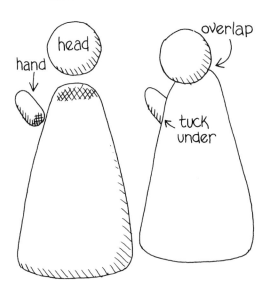

To make the headpiece, flatten a piece of uncolored dough and shape it as shown in the drawing. Make sure the headpiece curves around and covers the head and back. Brush water on the back of the headpiece and press it into position on the head and robe. Decorate the headpiece with tiny balls of light green dough and a little piece of light green rope.

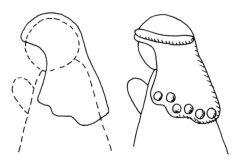

Leave the figure on the waxed paper either until the top seems dry or until the figure begins to curl; transfer it carefully, on a spatula, to a wire rack to finish drying.

4. Make two angels.

You will need some pale peach dough (uncolored dough plus a tiny bit of red and yellow paste food coloring) and small amounts of skin-color, pale yellow, red, dark brown and uncolored dough.

Work on a piece of waxed paper.

Transfer the patterns to thin cardboard to make templates as explained on page 12.

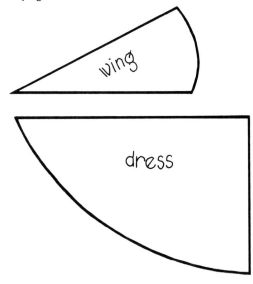

To make the dresses, roll out some pale peach dough to ⅛″ thick. Place the dress template on the dough, hold it lightly and cut around it. Turn the template over and repeat to make the second dress. Flatten the pointed end of each dress to prepare it for the head.

To make the wings, roll out some uncolored dough to ⅛″ thick. Place the wing template on the dough, hold it lightly and cut around it. Turn the template over and repeat to make the second wing. Flatten the pointed ends of the wings. Brush water on the edge of each wing and press gently but firmly to attach one to each dress.

Make a head for each angel: Roll a small ball of skin-color dough and flatten it to make a round, about 1″ in diameter. Brush water on the flattened parts of the dress and wing and press the head into position.

Make a halo for each angel: Roll a pale yellow rope about ³⁄₁₆″ in diameter and 3″ long. Flatten the ends, brush water on them and tuck them under the head. Shape the rope into a halo.

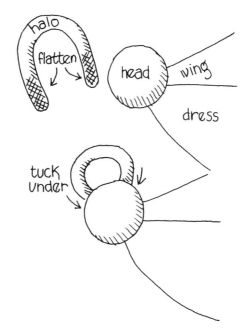

To make the features on each angel, roll a thin rope of dark brown dough for the hair, a tiny rope of red dough for the mouth and two tiny balls of uncolored dough for the eyes. Brush water on the face and press the features in position, following the photograph on page 121 for guidance in placement.

Leave the angels on the waxed paper until the tops seem dry; transfer to a wire rack to finish drying. If the wings or heads fall off during the transfer, don't worry. Simply realign them for now on the wire rack; later they can be reattached with Sobo glue.

5. Make two sheep and two lambs.

You will need uncolored dough plus a tiny bit of medium brown dough.

Roll out the uncolored dough to ⅛" thick. Use the cookie cutters to cut two sheep and two lambs. Place them on waxed paper, turning one sheep and one lamb over to face the opposite direction.

Brush water on one sheep. Force a small piece of dough through the garlic press until the strands are just ⅛" long or a bit longer. Use the small spatula to slice the strands off the garlic press and transfer them to the sheep. Press the strands very lightly to adhere them to the sheep. Make more strands and use them to cover the entire sheep *except for the face and feet.* **NOTE:** A toothpick may be helpful in this operation. Repeat the process for the remaining sheep and lambs. Clean the garlic press immediately.

Roll and flatten tiny balls of medium brown dough for the noses and feet. Brush with water and press each nose and foot in position on the sheep and lambs. Make eyes with the blunt end of a wooden skewer.

Leave the sheep and lambs on the waxed paper either until the tops seem dry or until the dough begins to curl; transfer them to a wire rack to finish drying.

6. Make two horses.

You will need light brown and dark brown dough.

Roll out the light brown dough to ⅛" thick. Use the cookie cutter to cut two horses. Place them on waxed paper, turning one horse over to face the opposite direction.

Brush the mane, the tail and the feet of each horse with water. Force a small piece of dark brown dough through the garlic press until the strands are about ½" long. Use a toothpick or wooden skewer to transfer them three or four at a time to the mane and tail. Press gently to adhere. Roll small balls of dark brown dough and press one in place on each foot. Make eyes with the blunt end of a wooden skewer.

Leave the horses on the waxed paper either until the tops seem dry or until the dough begins to curl; transfer to a wire rack to finish drying.

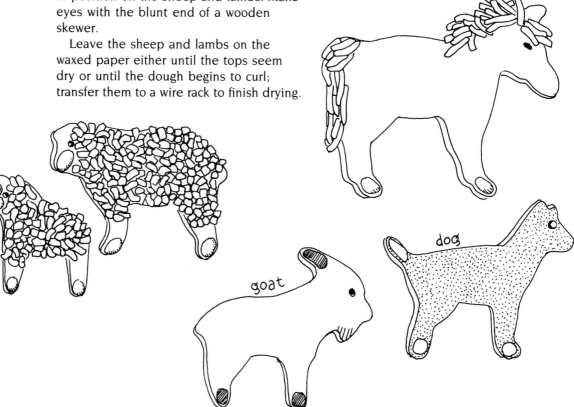

7. Make one cow, two goats and one dog.

You will need reddish brown dough, tan dough, a little uncolored dough and a tiny bit of medium brown dough.

Roll out the reddish brown dough to ⅛" thick. Use cookie cutters to cut one cow and one dog. Transfer them to waxed paper, with the cow facing left and the dog facing right.

Brush water on the cow. Shape small bits of uncolored dough to make the spots, eye, feet and the tip of the tail; press each one in position on the cow. Brush water on the dog. Shape small bits of uncolored dough to make the eye, tail and feet; press each one in position on the dog.

Roll out the tan dough to ⅛" thick. Use the cookie cutter to cut two goats. Transfer them to waxed paper, turning one goat over to face the opposite direction.

Brush water on each goat; shape small bits of medium brown dough to make the horns and the feet. Use the blunt end of a wooden skewer to make the eyes and the pointed end to make lines for the beards.

Leave all the animals on the waxed paper either until the tops seem dry or until the dough begins to curl up; transfer them to a wire rack to finish drying.

8. Make the star and the rays.

You will need a little bit of bright yellow dough and a little pale yellow dough.

Roll out the bright yellow dough to ⅛" thick and use the cookie cutter to cut a star. Roll out the pale yellow dough to ⅛" thick in a long strip. Use a sharp knife to cut four strips, each ⅛" wide and 2¾" long. **NOTE:** Cut a few extra rays so you can pick out the straightest ones.

Place the star and rays on waxed paper to dry.

9. Make the mosaic tiles.

You will need some bright yellow dough, some green dough and some red dough.

Roll out each color of dough to ⅛" thick. Cut it carefully in ½" squares. You will need 30 yellow tiles, 26 green ones and 22 red ones. **NOTE:** Make a few extra of each color so you can choose the best.

Place the tiles on waxed paper to dry, turning occasionally.

10. Make the foamcore background.

Cut the foamcore into two pieces, each 10" × 30". Cut each piece into three small pieces, as shown by the broken lines in the drawing. Use the mat knife or single-edge razor blade and work carefully on a big sheet of scrap cardboard.

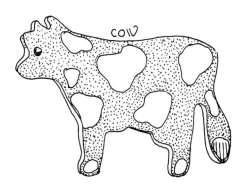

cow

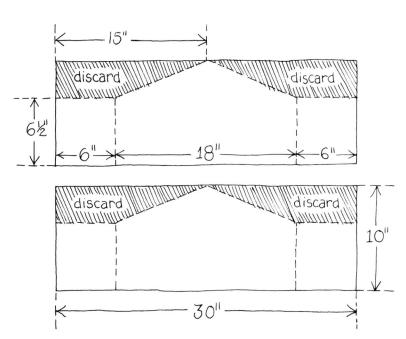

Glue the pieces together in identical pairs, spreading Sobo glue in a thin coat all the way to the edge of one of each pair. Weight each pair with books while the glue dries.

When the glue is completely dry, paint all three pieces. Mix the paint in a small jar; you'll need a good amount of it to give the foamcore several coats. The paint should be fairly thick, like heavy cream. Brush it on in wide strokes (back and edges, too) and let each coat dry before applying the next.

When the paint is thoroughly dry, attach the three pieces to make the triptych: Place the small pieces on the large piece, lining up the side and bottom edges as shown in the drawing. Work on the left side first: Apply glue sparingly but thoroughly to the left side edges and smooth one 7"-long piece of satin ribbon over the glue. Slip a sheet of waxed paper between the block of small pieces and the large piece, sliding the waxed paper all the way to the ribbon; this prevents the large and small foamcore pieces from sticking to each other if excess glue spreads between them. Let the glue dry. Repeat this process on the right side.

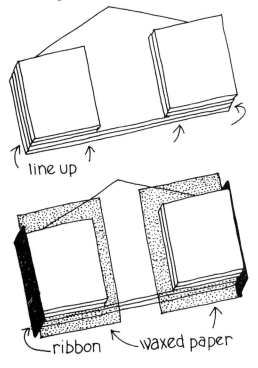

line up

ribbon   waxed paper

When the glue is dry, trim off any excess ribbon at the bottom and top. Remove the waxed paper, open the triptych out and stand it up. **NOTE:** It will not fold up flat after the figures and animals are glued to it.

11. Glue all the dough pieces to the background.

When all the dough pieces are completely dry (which may take several days), glue them to the foamcore background, following the photograph on page 121 for guidance. Arrange all the pieces in the correct positions, with the feet of the animals and people about 1" above the bottom edge of the triptych. Note that the sheep on the left overlaps the dog and the sheep on the right overlaps the horse. Add the angels, star, rays and mosaic tiles. When everything is arranged to your satisfaction, lift each piece, apply glue to the back (or at the points where it touches the background) and replace it in position.

Let the glue dry thoroughly.

12. Add the straw.

When the glue is dry on the animals and people, glue bits and pieces of packing straw to the blue background below and around their feet. The straw must be glued to the background piece by piece; there is no shortcut. Here's how to do it:

Break the straw into short lengths. Use tweezers to dip the back of each piece in a little puddle of glue and place it carefully on the background. Work across the background from left to right, making a thin layer of pieces of straw; it will not cover the background completely. Let it dry.

Repeat this process two more times, filling in most of the empty spaces. Now pick out lots of curly, loopy bits of straw and glue them over the previous layers. Let the glue dry.

Miniature Ornaments Tree

If you're lucky enough to have a small, live evergreen tree, these ornaments (shown actual size in the drawing) are the perfect decorations for it. Just add garlands, small balls and tiny lights, and you'll have a wonderful tabletop tree that will look charming in the entryway of your home, in the children's room, in the kitchen or even on your desk at work.

Once you get going, you'll find you can make many of these ornaments quickly, so plan to make several dozen.

Photograph, page 129, for design and color guidance

1. Color the dough.

Color small amounts of dough (see page 23), depending on your favorite colors and how many ornaments you plan to make. Refer to the photograph on page 129 for guidance in deciding what colors to make. Wrap each color tightly in plastic.

2. Prepare the paper clip loops.

Use the wire cutter to make several dozen paper clip loops. (See page 13 for instructions.) Set them aside to use as you make the ornaments. Make more as you need them.

3. Make the ornaments.

General instructions: Make five ornaments at a time, then make five more and so on. Roll out the dough for the birds and all the foundation pieces (large diamond, plain round, large scalloped round, large star) to ⅛" thick. Roll out the dough for the small diamond, heart, small scalloped round and small star to less than ⅛" thick. Insert a paper clip loop in each ornament as you make it. Set all ornaments on waxed paper to dry.

MATERIALS

Bread/glue dough (page 22)

Paste food colors (red, green, blue, yellow, orange)

Cookie cutters: scalloped rounds, 1⅛"–1¼" in diameter and ¾" in diameter; plain round, 1⅛"–1¼" in diameter; heart, 1"–1⅛" across; star, about 1⅛" across; small bird, about 1⅝" wide

Star-shaped aspic cutter

Paper clips (regular size), wire cutter

Red yarn, 4-ply or worsted-weight

Wire ornament hangers

Scalloped round: Use the cookie cutters to cut a large scalloped round in one color of dough and a small scalloped round in a different color. Brush water on the back of the small round and press it in place in the center of the large round. Roll a small ball of a different-colored dough and press it on the small round with a dab of water.

Plain round with heart: Use the cookie cutters to cut a plain round in one color of dough and a heart in another color. Brush water on the back of the heart and press it in place in the center of the round.

Star: Use the cookie cutter and the star-shaped aspic cutter to cut one large star and one small star in the same color of dough. Brush water on the back of the small star and press it in place in the center of the large star.

Bird: Use the cookie cutter to cut a bird. Using a second color of dough, shape a small wing and roll a tiny ball for the eye. Attach them to the bird with dabs of water.

Diamond: Use a sharp knife to cut a large diamond in one color of dough and a small diamond in another color. The drawing shows the approximate sizes of the diamonds. Brush water on the back of the small diamond and press it in place in the center of the large diamond.

4. Add the finishing touches.

When the ornaments are completely dry, tie a little yarn bow to one side of each paper clip loop. Hook an ornament hanger at the top of each paper clip loop and bend the end of the hanger as shown in the drawing.

Cookie Train

Each car of this holiday train is a pair of cookies sandwiched together with icing and decorated with piped and painted designs and small candies. In our photograph, page 129, we set the train upright by leaning each car against a wall or small box. You might prefer to arrange the train flat on a table, sideboard or pretty tray.

Photograph, page 129, for design and color guidance

1. Make and bake the basic cars for the train.

Since each car (engine, two freight cars, caboose) is made up of a pair of cookies sandwiched together with icing, you must cut two of each cookie for each car. For the engine, cut one cookie facing left and a second cookie facing right. (Turn the template over when you cut the second engine.)

Transfer the patterns to thin cardboard to make templates as explained on page 12.

On the flour-dusted back of a jelly roll pan, roll out half a recipe of dough to ¼″ thick. Place two templates on the dough, at least 1½″ apart. Cut away the dough between them as shown in the drawing.

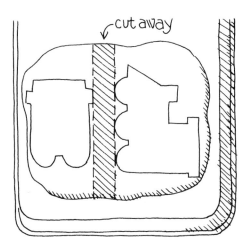

Hold each template lightly and cut around it with a sharp knife, removing the excess dough as you cut and wiping the knife often with a paper towel. Gather up the excess dough, knead it together lightly and refrigerate it for rerolling later. If there is room at the opposite end of the jelly roll pan, roll out more dough; if not, roll out half a recipe of dough on a second jelly roll pan and repeat the process to cut two more cookies. Bake the cookies according to the recipe, for 12–15 minutes. Watch the cookies carefully after 12 minutes; the edges should brown but the cookies remain light-colored on top.

Repeat this process to cut out and bake all the cookies required to make the cars. Let each cookie cool for five minutes on the jelly roll pan before moving it to a wire rack to finish cooling.

2. Make and bake the wheels for the cars.

On the flour-dusted back of a jelly roll pan, roll out some chilled dough to ¼″ thick. Use the cookie cutter to cut nine rounds, leaving 1½″ between the rounds. Lift away the excess dough. Find a glass with a flat bottom; dip the bottom in flour and use it to flatten each round to ⅛″ thick. Bake for eight to ten minutes; watch the wheels carefully after eight minutes, to be sure they do not get too brown. Cool the wheels on a wire rack.

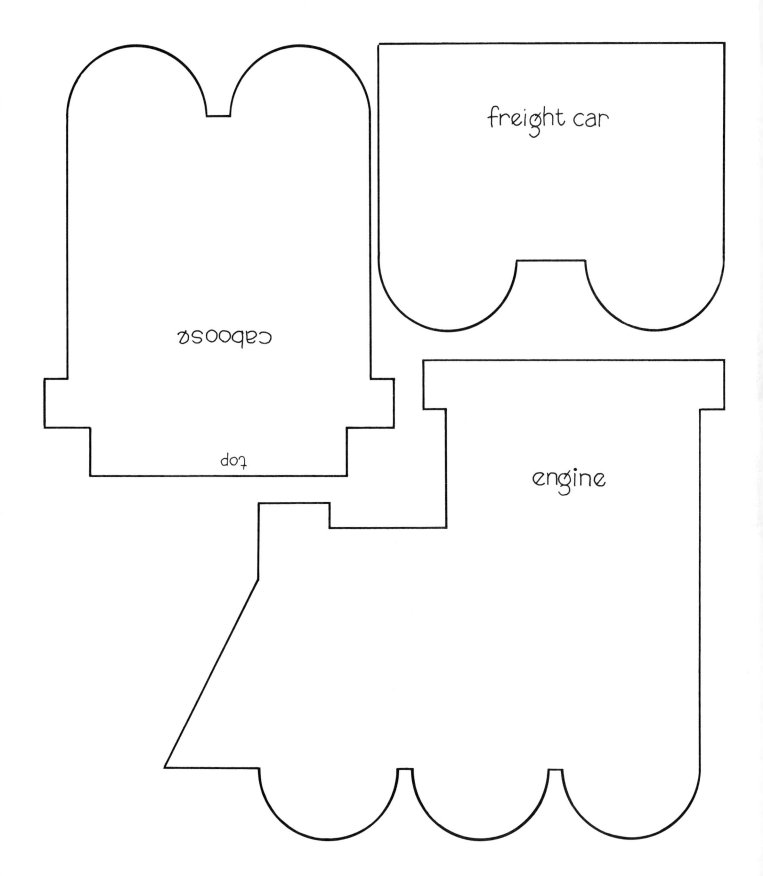

freight car

caboose

top

engine

3. Put the cookies together with icing.

To make each car, spread icing on the wrong side of one cookie and press the wrong side of a matching cookie against it, lining up the edges. Spread a little icing on the wrong side of each wheel and press it in position on a car, following the drawing and photograph (page 129) for guidance in placement. Let the icing dry for ten minutes.

4. Prepare the icing for decorating the train.

If you look closely at the photograph on page 129, you will see that the decorations on the trains are made with piped icing as well as icing that is painted on larger areas.

Put half a cup of white icing in a small bowl and add red food color to make bright red icing. Put all but a teaspoon of the red icing into a decorating bag fitted with a #2 tip. Mix the remaining teaspoon of red icing with half a teaspoon of water to make the paint. Cover tightly with plastic wrap.

Put half a cup of white icing in a small bowl and color it bright green. Put the green icing in a decorating bag fitted with a #2 tip.

Fill the third decorating bag (#2 tip) with white icing. Put a teaspoon of white icing in a small bowl and mix with half a teaspoon of water to make white paint. Cover tightly with plastic wrap.

5. Pipe white and red outlines and fill in with paint.

Following the diagram below, use the white icing and #2 icing tip to make white outlines and stripes on the train. Refer to the photograph on page 129 for additional guidance. Let the icing dry for a few minutes.

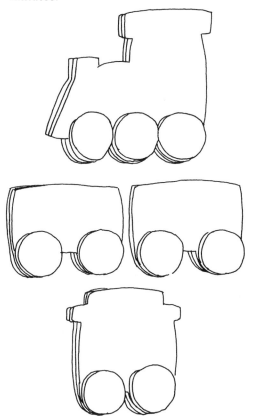

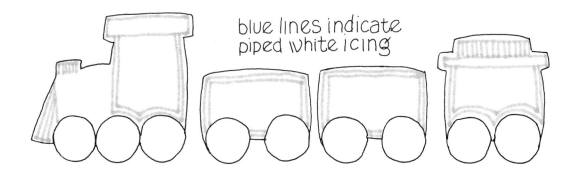

blue lines indicate piped white icing

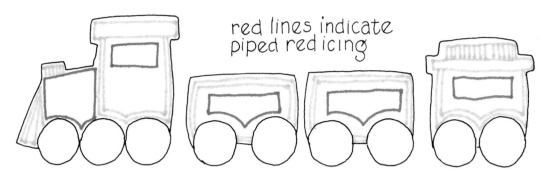

red lines indicate
piped red icing

Following the diagram above, use the red icing and #2 icing tip to make red outlines on the train. Let the icing dry for a few minutes.

Using the soft brush and white paint, fill in the engine roof and the caboose roof. Rinse the brush in water and then use the red paint to fill the areas within the red outlines. Let the paint dry.

Take up the bag of white icing again and pipe white outlines around the red outlines, except on the front part of the engine. Let the icing dry for a few minutes.

6. Decorate the wheels and add the final piped decorations.

With the green icing and #2 icing tip, pipe the spokes on the first wheel and then press a red candy in the center to make the hub.

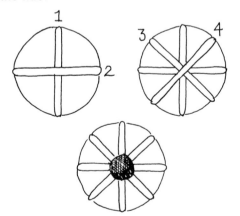

Repeat this process on the other eight wheels. Go back to the first wheel and pipe a green outline around the edge of the wheel. Continuing with the green icing, pipe the number 25 on the engine and then pipe a dot of green on each corner of the white outlines around the red areas.

With the red icing and #2 tip, pipe dots close to the hub of each wheel. Pipe red dots above and below the number 25.

Remove the #2 tip from the bag of white icing and replace it with the #27 tip. Pipe little flowers between the spokes of each wheel. Pipe one white flower on each side of the number 25 and, when they have dried, pipe a green dot on each one.

7. Add the candy decorations.

Attach four red candies to the train: Pipe a little red icing on the back of each candy and press one in place in the center of the engine roof, one in the center of each freight car and the last one in the center of the caboose roof.

Use a sharp knife to cut green gumdrops into 23 thin slices.

Attach the gumdrop slices: Pipe a little green icing on the back of each slice and press into position, following the photograph on page 129.

Let the icing dry overnight.

Santa, Mrs. Santa, Elves and Christmas Gifts

1 recipe of gingerbread dough (page 27)

Cookie cutters: gingerbread man and woman, each about 5" high; miniature gingerbread boy and girl

½ recipe of decorator icing (page 29)

Paste food colors (red, green)

3 decorating bags

3 #2 icing tips

#27, #33 and #46 icing tips, one of each

Assorted colors of imperials (little round candies)

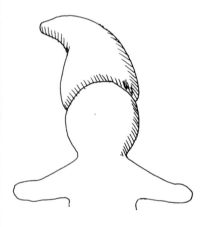

You don't have to make a special snow scene for your cookies like the one we made for the photograph—just serve up Santa, Mrs. Santa and as many elves and gifts as you like on any pretty plate or tray.

Photograph, page 135, for design and color guidance

1. Make and bake the basic cookies.

Sprinkle flour generously on the work surface and roll out half the chilled dough on it. Use the cookie cutters to make one man (Santa, of course), one woman (Mrs. Santa) and a flock of miniature boys and girls (the elves). Transfer to a cookie sheet, leaving about 1" between cookies. Gather up the excess dough and roll it into a ball, saving a bit of it to use for Santa's hat. Shape the hat and press it gently into position.

Knead the excess dough into a smooth ball, wrap it in plastic and return it to the refrigerator.

Bake the cookies according to the recipe; watch the small cookies carefully, since they may be finished baking before the large ones.

When the cookie sheet is available again (or if you have a second cookie sheet), roll out the remaining dough and cut some 1"–2" squares and rectangles for the gifts. You may also want to make extra Santas, Mrs. Santas and elves so there won't be any squabbling.

2. Prepare the icing.

Divide the icing in three equal parts. Put one third (white) right into a decorating bag with a #2 icing tip and place each of the other parts into a small bowl. Color one bowl of icing red and the other green. Put the red icing into a second decorating bag with a #2 tip and the green icing into a third bag with a #2 tip. Keep the #27, #33 and #46 tips handy.

3. Decorate the cookies.

Work in a sort of assembly line, piping as much with each color and icing tip as possible before moving on to the next color and tip. There may be some backtracking, but you will find that the piping goes quickly by this method. Follow the steps below, leaving the faces and gifts for last.

1. Pipe the white lines and dots on Mrs. Santa and one third of the elves. Let the icing dry for a few minutes.

2. Pipe the green lines and dots on Santa, Mrs. Santa and another third of the elves. The only green dots you can't do right now are the dots on Santa's buttons. Let the icing dry for a few minutes.

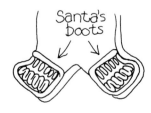

3. Pipe the red lines and dots on Santa, Mrs. Santa and the remaining third of the elves. Let the icing dry for a few minutes.

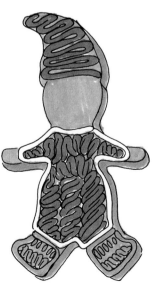

4. Change the tip on the bag of white icing to a #27 and pipe the flowers for Mrs. Santa's hair. (See photograph on page 135).

5. Change the tip on the bag of white icing to a #33 and pipe the edging of Santa's hat and the edgings and buttons of Santa's suit. Pipe one flower on the tip of the hat. **NOTE:** If you don't have a #33 tip, use the #27.

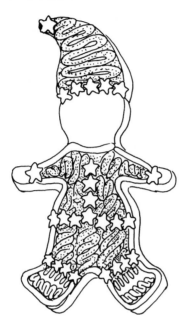

6. Add the border of red candies to Mrs. Santa's skirt: Using the #2 tip on the bag of white icing, pipe dots across the skirt and press one candy on each dot.

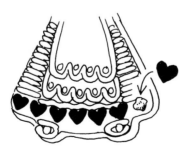

7. Return to the green icing with the #2 tip and pipe dots on Santa's buttons. (See photograph on page 135.)

8. Line up all the cookies (except the gifts) and pipe all the faces at one time, using #2 tips on all three decorating bags; pipe hair on the elves. (See photograph on page 135.)

9. Add Santa's eyebrows, moustache and beard. (See photograph on page 135.)

10. Change the tip on the bag of white icing to a #46 and pipe crossed lines on one third of the gifts. Repeat with the red and green icing. Let the icing dry for a few minutes.

11. Put the #2 tips on all three bags of icing and pipe bows on the gifts, pressing a round candy in the center of each bow. (See photograph on page 135.)

Gingerbread Christmas Tree

The ornaments on this delicious tree are little gingerbread cookies attached with icing and decorated with painted and piped icing.

Photograph, page 138, for design and color guidance

1. Make and bake the gingerbread tree and ornaments.

Enlarge the half-pattern, make a full-size whole pattern and transfer it to thin cardboard to make a template as explained on page 12.

On the flour-dusted back of a jelly roll pan, roll out the dough to ¼" thick. Place the template on the dough, hold it lightly and cut around it with a sharp knife. Lift away the excess dough and transfer the excess dough to a floured surface.

Bake the tree according to the recipe, leaving it in the oven longer than eight to ten minutes if necessary.

While the tree is baking, use the cookie cutters to cut the ornaments from the excess rolled dough: one large star; 29 small stars; ten leaves; two birds (turn one over to face the opposite direction); four hearts; one diamond. **NOTE:** It's a good idea to cut out one or two extras of each shape, just in case you drop one or someone happens to pop one into his mouth.

Bake the ornaments according to the recipe. Watch the smallest pieces carefully and take them out of the oven as soon as they are done.

2. Make a foamcore base for the tree.

The foamcore base will allow you to move the tree around easily.

Place the cooled gingerbread tree on the foamcore and draw around it with

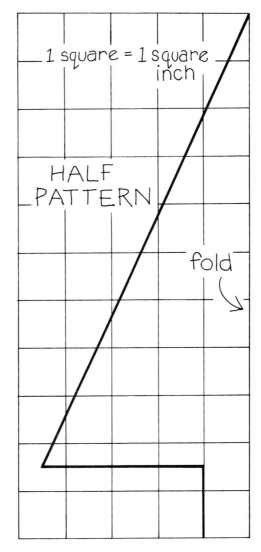

1 square = 1 square inch

HALF PATTERN

fold

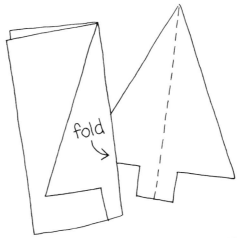

fold

MATERIALS

1 recipe of gingerbread dough (page 27)

Cookie, canapé and aspic cutters: star, 1¾" wide; star-shaped aspic cutter; leaf-shaped aspic cutter; bird, about 2" wide; heart, about 1¼" wide and 1" high; diamond, about 2¼" wide and 3½" high

Foamcore, one piece about 9½" × 11½"

Mat knife or X-acto® knife

½ recipe of decorator icing (page 29)

Paste food colors (red, green, blue, yellow)

Small, soft brush for painting icing on the cookies

3 decorating bags

3 #2 icing tips

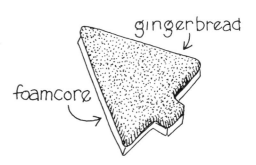

pencil. Remove the gingerbread tree carefully and cut out the foamcore tree shape with the mat knife or X-acto® knife. To attach the two trees, spread some icing on the foamcore tree and press the gingerbread tree onto it, matching the edges. Let the icing dry.

3. Prepare the icing for decorating the ornaments and tree.

There are three steps to decorating the gingerbread tree: A) paint color on the ornament cookies; B) attach the ornaments to the tree; C) pipe lines and dots on the

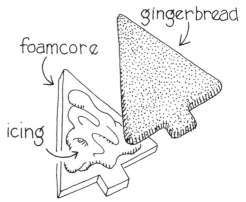

ornaments and on the tree. Before carrying out these steps, prepare the icing needed for them.

To make the paint, put one teaspoon of icing into each of five cups of a gem muffin tin. Add ½ teaspoon of water to each cup of icing and mix well to make a consistency slightly thicker than heavy cream. Leave one gem cup of icing white; use paste food colors to make the other cups red, green, blue and yellow. Cover the muffin tin tightly with plastic wrap.

Put a #2 icing tip on each of the decorating bags. Divide the remaining icing in thirds. Color one third red, one third green and leave the last third white. Put one color into each decorating bag.

4. Paint the ornament cookies.

First arrange the ornament cookies on the gingerbread tree, picking out the best ones and setting aside the extras. Place the chosen ornaments on a piece of waxed paper and set aside the gingerbread tree for now.

Take the plastic wrap off the gem muffin tin and practice painting an extra cookie. Let the paint flow off the soft brush to make a thick coat on the top surface of the cookie; don't let the paint drip down the sides of the cookie. Paint the ornament cookies in the following order: stars, yellow; birds, blue; hearts, red; leaves, green; diamond, white. Rinse the brush in clean water before changing paint colors.

Let the first coat dry thoroughly—it is quite sticky and may take an hour to dry. Paint a second coat on each cookie and let that dry thoroughly before proceeding to step 5.

5. Attach the ornaments to the tree.

Arrange the painted stars correctly on the gingerbread tree. Lift each small star (including the one on the large star), pipe a dot of white icing on the back and replace it in position. Lift the large star, pipe several dots of icing on the back and replace it in position. Let the icing dry for a few minutes.

Arrange all the remaining ornament cookies on the tree in the correct design. Lift each one (in this order: diamond; birds; hearts; leaves), pipe dots or lines of white icing on the back and replace in position on the tree. Let the icing dry for several minutes.

6. Pipe lines and dots on the ornaments and on the tree.

Work with one color at a time, following the order below and checking the photograph on page 138 for guidance.

White icing: Pipe one dot on each small star and a dot on each point of the large star. Pipe a border of dots on the trunk of the tree. Pipe an eye, wing and tail feathers on each bird.

Green icing: Pipe a center line on each leaf and several dots on the trunk of the tree. Fill in the wing of each bird. Pipe the word NOEL on the diamond, drawing the letters first with the tip of a knife or toothpick. Pipe a dot on each point of the diamond. Finally, make curlicues and dots directly on the gingerbread tree.

Red icing: Outline each heart. Pipe a border of dots around the edge of the diamond and three dots on the letter *O*. Pipe dots directly on the gingerbread tree, near the green curlicues.

Green icing again: Pipe a dot on each heart.
Let the icing dry.

Cookie Tree

140

MATERIALS

3 recipes of cookie dough (page 27)

Small saucers, glasses, round cookie cutters or biscuit cutters with the following diameters: 5″; 4″; 3⅜″; 2¾″; 2″; 1½″; 1″

One recipe of decorator icing (page 29)

Paste food colors (red, blue)

2 decorating bags

#27 icing tip and #2 icing tip

Edible silver balls (available for cake decorations)

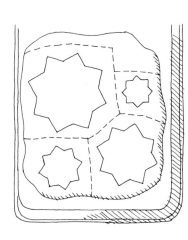

This pretty tree is composed of pairs of star-shaped cookies in graduated sizes, separated by pairs of round cookies in graduated but smaller sizes.

Photograph, page 142, for design and color guidance

1. Make and bake the star-shaped cookies.

Trace each half-pattern (#3–8) twice to make it into a whole pattern, using the dotted line as the center line.

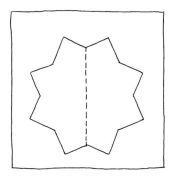

Transfer patterns #1–8 to thin cardboard to make templates as explained on page 12; make a separate template for each size, a total of eight templates.

On the flour-dusted back of a jelly roll pan, roll out half a recipe of dough at a time to ¼″ thick. Arrange several templates on the dough, leaving 1½″ between templates; try to place them in a space-saving arrangement. Cut between the templates to section them off from one another.

Hold each template lightly and cut around it with a sharp knife, lifting away the excess dough as you cut.

Bake the cookies according to the recipe; the smaller cookies will take less time to finish baking (perhaps five minutes) than the larger cookies (perhaps 12 minutes),

so watch them carefully and remove them as they are done. Let the cookies cool on wire racks.

Repeat the rolling, cutting and baking process to make two cookies of each size, a total of 16. For the top of the tree, cut one additional cookie with the 1″-diameter cookie cutter.

2. Make and bake the round divider cookies.

Pairs of round divider cookies will go between the pairs of star-shaped cookies in the final assembly of the cookie tree. Use your collection of eight round cookie cutters (sizes listed in the *Materials* section) to make these dividers.

On the flour-dusted back of a jelly roll pan, roll out half a recipe of dough at a time to ¼″ thick. Cut out two divider cookies of each size, fitting only as many as you can and leaving 1½″ between cookies. Lift away the excess dough as you cut.

Bake the cookies according to the recipe. Watch the cookies carefully and remove each one as it is done.

Repeat the rolling, cutting and baking process to make two divider cookies of each size, a total of 16.

3. Do the preliminary assembly of the cookies.

Now you have eight pairs of star-shaped cookies and eight pairs of round cookies plus one cookie for the top of the tree.

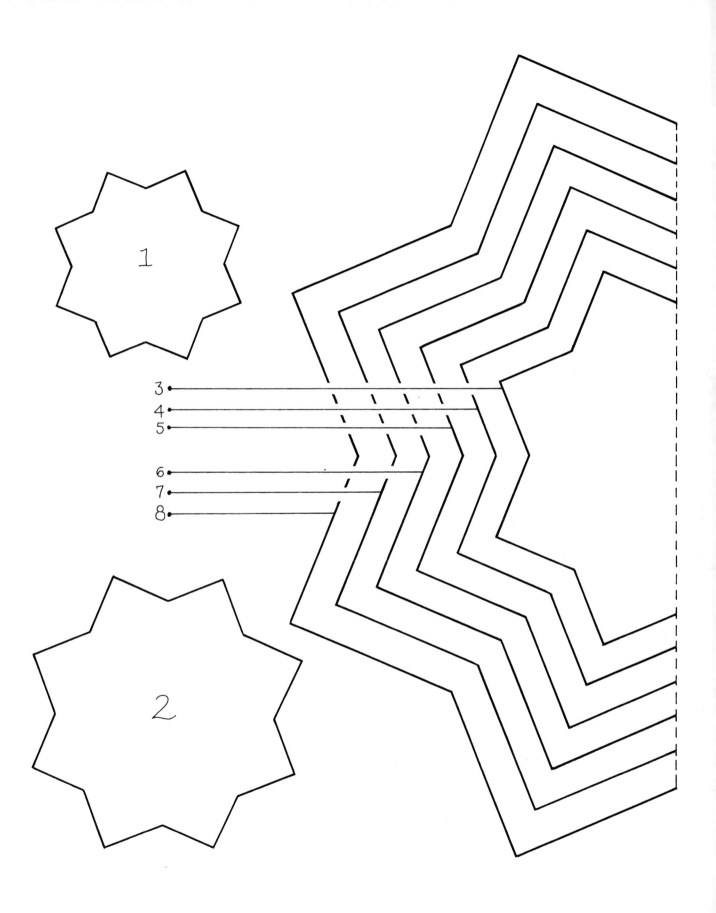

Spread icing about ⅛"–¼" thick between one pair of identical cookies, bringing the icing not quite to the edges. **NOTE:** Both cookies should be right side up. Press the two cookies together gently, lining up the edges. Work quickly because the icing dries quickly. Repeat for all the pairs of cookies.

right side

put together with icing

right side

Set aside the largest pair of round cookies for now. Center the remaining pairs of stars and rounds as shown in the drawing, spreading icing between each set of pairs. Do *not* make the final stack at this time. Let the icing dry.

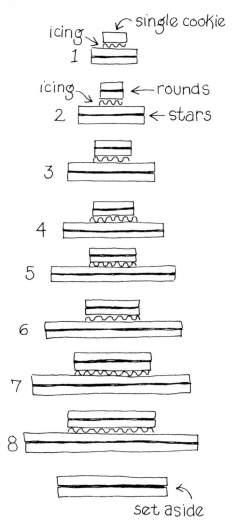

4. Decorate the star-shaped cookies.

Put about half a cup of icing in a small bowl and mix in a little red paste food color to make pink. Fit the #27 tip on one decorating bag and fill with pink icing. Put about half a cup of icing in another small bowl and add a bit of blue paste food color to make light blue. Fit the #2 tip on the other decorating bag and fill with blue icing. Pour the silver balls into a small bowl and keep the tweezers handy.

Start with the largest star-shaped cookie (#8): Pipe a pink flower at each point, topping each with a silver ball. I find it easiest to pipe four or five flowers at a time and place a silver ball on each one with tweezers. Repeat this process on star-shaped cookies #2–7; pipe eight flowers on star-shaped cookie #1 and a ring of five pink flowers on the smallest cookie.

Now pipe rows of blue dots between the pink flowers on all the star-shaped cookies. Pipe a small mound of blue icing in the center of the smallest cookie. Let all the icing dry overnight.

5. Do the final assembly of the cookie tree.

First choose a pretty plate or tray on which to assemble the tree; it must have a flat bottom large enough to accommodate the largest pair of round divider cookies. If you want to line the plate with a paper doily, anchor the doily by dabbing a little icing in a few spots on the plate and then centering the doily on the plate. Hold the doily in place until the icing sets.

Now spread a ⅛"-thick layer of white icing on the bottom of the largest pair of round cookies and press the pair, centered, on the plate (or doily). Let the icing dry for a few minutes so the cookies are secured.

Next spread a layer of icing, ⅛"–¼" thick, on the *top* of that same (largest) pair of round cookies, and immediately center the largest pair of star-shaped cookies (which are topped with a pair of round cookies) on the icing. Let the icing dry for a few minutes.

Repeat this process of spreading icing and centering the next pair of star-shaped cookies on top of the icing, to make a graduated stack, as shown in the photograph on page 142. **NOTE:** It is important to let each layer dry for a few minutes before adding the next. Even more important, check the stack from all sides to be sure it is straight and centered—and not becoming a leaning tower.

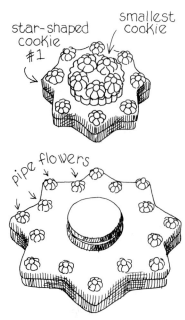

Leaf and Berry Candleholder (small size)

MATERIALS

Flour/salt dough (page 16)

Canapé cutter with straight sides, about 1" in diameter

Scalloped cookie cutter, about 2½" in diameter

Acrylic paints (white, blue, red, opaque silver); brushes

Polyurethane, brush, turpentine

Silver glitter

Each candleholder will accommodate a candle about ¾" in diameter. Use dripless candles to avoid getting wax on the candleholder. If some wax does drip on the candleholder, simply put it in the freezer for a few hours and then break off the bits of chilled wax.

Photograph, page 142, for design and color guidance

1. Make the foundation.

As you see in the photograph on page 142, the leaves and berries of the candleholder are supported by a simple foundation.

Apply a thin film of vegetable oil to the outside of the canapé cutter and place the cutter upside down on a cookie sheet. Roll a rope of dough ¾" in diameter and 8" long. Wrap it loosely around the canapé cutter and cut off the excess dough. Join the ends of the rope with water, neatly smoothing the joint. Leave the canapé cutter in place.

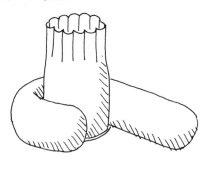

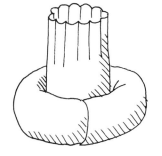

2. Make the leaves and attach them to the foundation.

Make no more than five leaves at a time.

Roll out some dough to ¼" thick. Make each leaf with the scalloped cookie cutter, cutting out one side first and then moving the cutter over to cut the other side. The leaf should measure about 1½" from point to point. Use the back of a knife blade to make a deep indentation for the center line; be careful not to cut all the way through the dough.

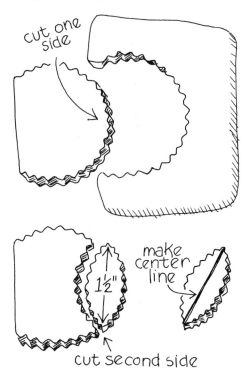

Brush water onto a 1"-wide section of the foundation. Place a leaf on the water, at an angle, with the tip of the leaf just short of the canapé cutter. Press gently to adhere. Now brush water on the left edge of the leaf and on another inch of the foundation. Place a second leaf overlapping the first leaf about ¼″. Press gently to adhere it to the first leaf and the foundation.

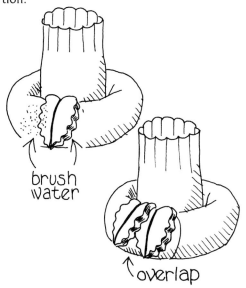

brush water

overlap

Continue in this manner, working all the way around the foundation. Tuck the left edge of the last leaf under the right edge of the first leaf.

3. Make the berries and attach them to the leaves.

Each berry is a ball of dough about ⅝″ in diameter. Make ten berries; you may need one more or one less.

Brush water sparingly along the upper ends of the leaves. Place as many berries as needed to make a ring, brushing water sparingly between the berries, too. The last berry should close the ring. Make a shallow hole in each berry, using the pointed end of a paint brush.

make shallow holes

brush water between berries

4. Bake the candleholder.

Bake the candleholder at 250° for an hour and then run a spatula under it to loosen it from the cookie sheet. Continue baking until it seems to be done. Turn off the heat and leave the candleholder in the oven overnight. Remove it from the oven. Take out the canapé cutter by pulling it down gently.

5. Paint and polyurethane the candleholder.

Paint the candleholder white, inside and out. When the white is dry, paint two coats of pink (white paint with a little red mixed in) on the berries, letting each coat dry thoroughly. Paint the sides and the center lines of the leaves medium blue and let the paint dry. Brush the tops of the leaves with a lighter blue. When the light blue is dry, use a thin brush to paint medium blue strokes on the right half of each leaf. (Check the photograph on page 142 for guidance.) Paint the foundation (including the bottom) with two coats of silver. When all the paint is dry, go back and do any touch-ups that may be necessary.

Brush one coat of polyurethane on the tops of the berries and sprinkle with silver glitter. Let the polyurethane dry. Brush two coats of polyurethane over the entire candleholder, letting each coat dry completely before applying the next.

Here are five wall decorations to make, from the simple (framed mosaics) to the challenging (The Night Before Christmas). Whichever of the five you make, I think you'll be so proud of your doughcraft wall decoration that you'll want to take down one of your year-round wall pieces—like a painting, photograph or mirror—and replace it with your doughcraft creation for the duration of the holiday season. When the holidays are over, carefully wrap and store the doughcraft wall decoration—and bring it out again next year.

The Night Before Christmas Wall Piece

MATERIALS

Flour/salt dough (page 16)

Light brown cork bulletin board (framed in flat, wood molding), 12″ high and 18″ wide

3½ yards satin ribbon, ⅛″ wide, for the floor lines

527 cement

Acrylic paints (white, assorted colors); brushes

Scalloped cookie cutter, 2½″ in diameter

Plain or scalloped round cookie cutter, 1¼″ in diameter

Plain or scalloped round cookie cutter, 1″ in diameter

Polyurethane, brush, turpentine

Trims and decorations: narrow (about ½″-wide) gold garland; bits of baby rickrack, ⅛″-wide ribbon and thin gold cord; gold sequins-on-a-string; red plastic beads, about ⅜″ in diameter; tiny cloth flowers cut from a bunch of artificial flowers; tiny pearl beads; little red glass beads (for the berries on the wreath)

2 yards grosgrain ribbon, ⅜″ wide, for the frame

Gold trim for the frame
NOTE: Use any relatively flat type of sewing or craft trim. It must be narrow enough to be centered comfortably on the wood molding of your frame.

Photograph, page 146, for design and color guidance

Anyone who loves miniatures will love making this wall piece. You don't need any special skills, but a steady hand will help with the details of the painting. If you don't have a particularly steady hand, simply omit the more delicate painting—the stripes on the stockings and the flowers on the clock.

The plaque is made on a framed cork bulletin board. Mine is 12″ high and 18″ wide—but if you must buy some other size, your plaque can be done just as successfully if you make some slight alterations in the directions as you go along. For example, on a wider bulletin board you may need a few extra little packages or candy canes to fill out the floor. Or you may find, on a smaller bulletin board, that it is too crowded with a tree, a fireplace and a clock, so you might want to eliminate the clock.

Unless your bulletin board is radically different in size, the best plan is to make and bake all the dough pieces and arrange them in the frame—and then decide if you have too many, too few or just the right amount.

1. Make the floor of the little room.

With pencil, draw the floor line right on the cork bulletin board, 2⅞″ from the inside edge of the frame. Draw six more lines below it, evenly spaced, ⁷⁄₁₆″ apart. Note that the seventh line will be very close to the wood frame.

Cement pieces of ⅛″-wide satin ribbon along the pencil lines; be sure to line up the top edge of each ribbon with each pencil line. Trim the ends neatly at the left and right edges of the frame. Let the cement dry.

2. Paint the wall.

With the acrylic paints, mix a pale peach color (white plus a bit of red and a bit of yellow) and add water to make a thin wash. Apply the wash to the cork area above the floor, brushing an even coat right down to the floor line. Let the paint dry.

NOTE: Mix the pale peach paint a little lighter than you want it to be; when the wash dries it will look slightly darker because of the cork color underneath.

Draw vertical pencil lines every ¾″ across the wall, starting ¾″ from the left inside edge of the frame. Paint over the lines twice with light brown paint. Remember that the lines do not have to be perfect, so paint freehand—no rulers allowed.

Now paint simple pink flowers, evenly spaced, in the first vertical row. Each flower is five petals—five little brush strokes.

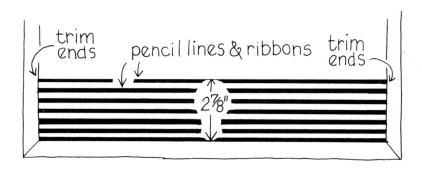

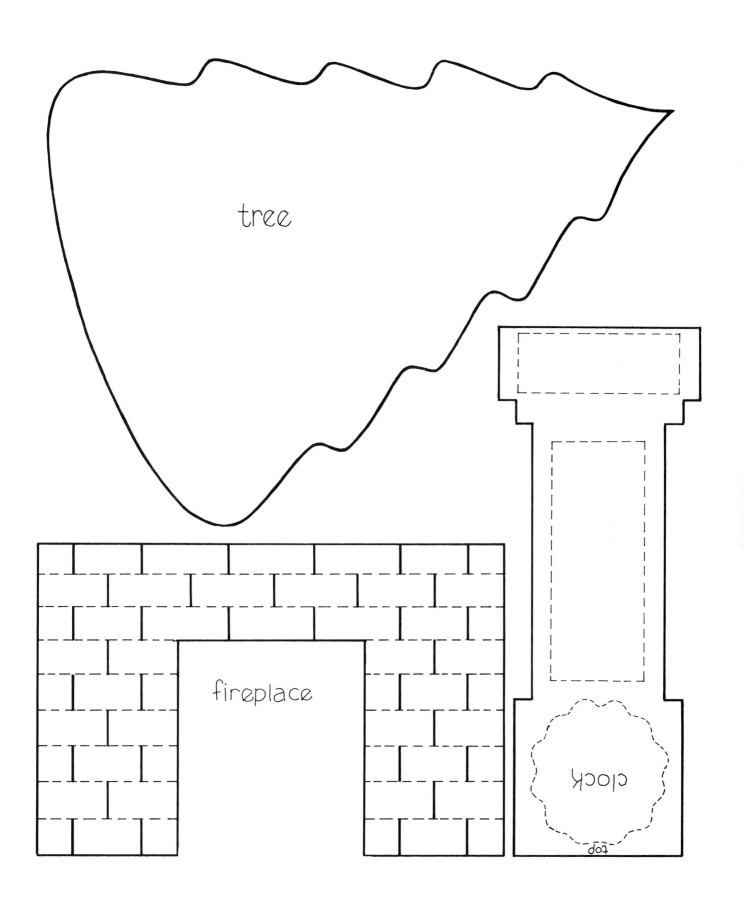

tree

fireplace

clock

top

149

Paint flowers in the second vertical row, spacing them to fall between those in the first row.

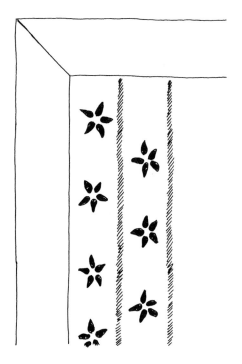

Continue painting flowers in all the vertical rows. The flowers in the odd rows are positioned like those in the first row; the flowers in the even rows are positioned like those in the second row. Refer to the photograph on page 146 for guidance.

Paint a red dot in the center of each flower. Paint several green leaves around each flower. Let the paint dry.

3. Make the Christmas tree.

Transfer all three patterns to thin cardboard to make templates as explained on page 12. Do not transfer the solid and dotted lines; they are for reference only.

Roll out some dough to 1/4" thick. Place the tree template on the dough, hold it lightly and cut around it with a sharp knife. Remove the excess dough as you cut. Use a spatula to lift the tree to a cookie sheet.

Now add three-dimensional texture to the basic tree: Brush water on the lower end of the tree. Roll small ovals of dough and press them in place in a row at the bottom of the tree, brushing more water on the tree if necessary. Flatten the top edge of each oval.

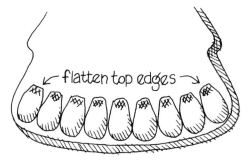

Make a second row of ovals, overlapping the ovals in the first row. Don't forget to flatten the top edge of each oval.

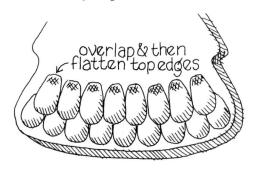

Continue making rows of ovals, working up to the top of the tree.

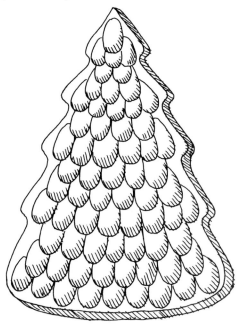

Leave the tree on the cookie sheet while you proceed to step 4.

4. Make the clock.

Roll out some dough to ¼″ thick. Place the clock template on the dough, hold it lightly and cut around it with a sharp knife. Remove the excess dough. Use a spatula to lift the clock to the cookie sheet.

Roll out some dough to ⅛″ thick. Cut out the clock face using the 1¼″-diameter plain or scalloped round cookie cutter. Cut out a rectangle 2½″ high and 1″ wide for the vertical panel of the clock and a rectangle ⅝″ high and 1¾″ wide for the horizontal panel of the clock. Brush the clock with water and press the parts in place, following the dotted lines on the pattern as a guide. Using the blunt end of a wooden skewer, incise holes on the clock as shown in the drawing.

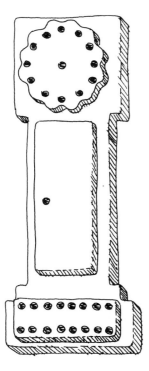

Leave the clock on the cookie sheet with the tree while you proceed to Step 5.

5. Make the fireplace.

Roll out some dough to ¼″ thick. Place the fireplace template on the dough, hold it lightly and cut around it with a sharp knife. Remove the excess dough. Carefully lift the fireplace to the cookie sheet. Use the template as a guide for resetting the shape of the fireplace.

Roll out some dough to a little more than ¼″ thick. Cut a strip about ¼″ high and a little wider than the fireplace. Brush water along the cut edge at the top of the fireplace and butt the strip against it to make the mantel.

Use the back of a knife blade to make the horizontal indentations for the bricks (shown by the dotted lines on the fireplace pattern). Make the vertical indentations for the bricks (shown by the short, solid lines on the pattern) with the rounded tip of a knife. Press the back of the blade firmly into the dough but be careful not to cut through the dough.

6. Bake the tree, clock and fireplace.

Bake the pieces at 250° for half an hour and then run a spatula under them to loosen them from the cookie sheet. Continue baking until they are completely hard. Do not turn over during baking. Remove from the oven and allow the pieces to cool.

7. Make all the smaller pieces and accessories.

Look carefully at the photograph on page 146 for guidance when making these miniatures.

Wreath: Roll out some dough to ¼" thick. Cut one round with the 2½"-diameter scalloped cookie cutter. Cut out the center of the wreath with the 1"-diameter round cookie cutter. Transfer to the cookie sheet.

Packages: Roll out some dough to ¼" thick. Use a sharp knife to cut out ten squares and rectangles in a variety of sizes; the smallest can be about ½" × 1" and the largest about 1¼" square. Transfer them to the cookie sheet.

Candy canes: Make two or three from scraps of rolled dough. For each candy cane, cut a strip ⅜" wide and 2¾" long. Transfer the strip to the cookie sheet. Round the edges and bend the strip into a candy cane shape.

Teddy bear: The teddy bear is made of balls of dough. For the body, roll a ball of dough 1" in diameter and flatten it slightly. For the head, roll a smaller ball, shape it as shown and attach to the body with a little water. Roll small balls for the ears and four paws, flattening each ball slightly before attaching it to the bear with water. Use the blunt end of a wooden skewer to make indentations in the ears and paws. Use the blunt and pointed ends to make the features. Transfer the bear to the cookie sheet.

Candles: Make two candles in candleholders. Cut the 1"-wide holders from scraps of rolled-out dough. For each candle, roll a short rope about ¼" in diameter, flatten it slightly and cut off a piece 1" long. Shape a little bit of dough for each flame. Put the parts together with water, working on the cookie sheet.

Stockings: Mold by hand two large ones and two small ones. Use the back of a knife blade to incise lines on the toes and heels and to simulate ribbing. Transfer to the cookie sheet.

Logs: To make the large log, roll a bit of dough into a rope about ⅜" in diameter. Break off the ends gently to make a piece about 1½" long. Flatten the piece slightly and make a few lines in it to simulate bark. To make two smaller logs, repeat the process using a rope of dough about ¼" in diameter. Transfer all three logs to the cookie sheet.

8. Bake all the small pieces.

Bake at 250° for 20 minutes and then run a spatula under all the pieces to loosen them from the cookie sheet. Some of the small pieces may be finished baking at this point, so check them and remove any that are completely hard. Continue baking the remaining pieces, watching them carefully to avoid burning. Remove each one as it is done.

9. Paint and polyurethane all the pieces.

Paint all the pieces with two coats of white, letting each coat dry thoroughly. Then paint each piece with two coats of color, referring to the photograph on page 146 for guidance.

When the paint is dry, brush two or three coats of polyurethane on each piece. Allow each coat to dry before applying the next.

10. Arrange the pieces and cement them to the background.

Arrange the pieces on the background, following the photograph on page 146. Discard any unnecessary pieces and then make a note or a little sketch of the arrangement of the packages.

Pick up each package and tie or wrap it with ⅛"-wide ribbon, gold cord or baby rickrack. (Attach the rickrack to the package with 527 cement.) Replace each package in position on the background, using your notes to remind you where each one goes.

Use 527 cement to adhere the pieces to the background, applying the cement to the back of each piece at the points where the piece will touch the background. Cement the following pieces in the following order: tree; fireplace; clock; packages; candy canes; teddy bear. Let the cement dry.

While the 527 is drying on the pieces listed, add some of the finishing touches: Wrap and cement narrow gold garland around the wreath. Cement a length of gold garland across the mantel and another little piece across the top of the clock. Shape a piece of gold garland into five equal scallops that reach across the background and cement it in place, as shown in the photograph on page 146. Let the 527 dry.

Now cement the wreath in place above the fireplace, the candles on each end of the mantel, the logs in the opening of the fireplace and the stockings on top of the fireplace.

11. Add the finishing touches.

Cement the little red glass beads to the wreath, referring to the photograph on page 146 for guidance.

Adhere the decorations to the tree: First cement five rows of gold sequins-on-a-string, starting with a short length near the top of the tree. Each row should be arranged in a wavy (not straight) line. Let the cement dry. Now arrange the tiny cloth flowers and the red plastic beads on the tree. When you have an arrangement you like, lift each bead and flower, apply 527 to the *tree* and replace the bead or flower in position. Cement a tiny pearl bead in the center of each flower. Make a little ball of narrow gold garland and cement it to the top of the tree.

Decorate the wood frame: Center and cement a piece of grosgrain ribbon on each side of the frame, mitering the ribbon at each corner. Center and cement a length of gold trim over each piece of ribbon, cutting neatly at the corners.

Merry Christmas Sign

MATERIALS

3-4 recipes of bread/glue dough (page 22)

Ruler, triangle

Paste food colors (red, green, yellow)

Christmas tree cookie cutter, about 2″ wide and 2¾″ high

Star cookie cutter, about 1¼″ across

Foamcore, ³⁄₁₆″ thick, one piece 26″ × 32″

Mat knife or single-edge razor blade

Acrylic paint (blue, white); soft, wide brush

Silver glitter

Acrylic gloss medium (a thick, whitish substance used both to dilute acrylic paints and as an adhesive; available where you buy acrylic paints)

Sobo glue

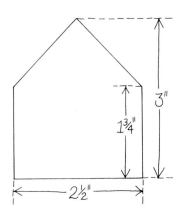

Photograph, page 155, for design and color guidance

1. Make the mosaic tiles needed for the letters.

Roll out one batch of uncolored dough to ⅛″ thick. Using a ruler and triangle for measuring, cut a rectangle of dough 5″ × 10″. Gather up and rewrap the excess dough. With the tip of a sharp knife, lightly mark the surface of the rectangle in ½″ squares, a total of 200 squares. Cut the squares apart with the knife and carefully transfer them to waxed paper to dry. As the squares dry, move them around on the waxed paper so they don't stick to it; turn the squares over once or twice so they dry evenly.

2. Make the houses and the doors for the houses.

Color one half of a recipe of dough bright red. Roll it out to ⅛″ thick and cut out three houses, following the diagram to the left.

Set the houses on waxed paper to dry. When the edges begin to dry and curl up, transfer the houses to a wire rack to finish drying.

Roll out a bit of uncolored dough to ⅛″ thick. Cut out three rectangles, each ¾″ wide and 1¼″ high, for the doors. Let them dry on waxed paper.

3. Make the trees and stars.

Color one half of a recipe of dough bright green. Roll it out to ⅛″ thick and use the tree cookie cutter to cut four trees. Place the trees on waxed paper to dry and then transfer them to wire racks when the edges begin to dry and curl up.

Color one recipe of dough bright yellow. Roll it out to ⅛″ thick and use the star cookie cutter to make 45 stars. Let them dry as described above.

4. Prepare the signboard.

While the dough pieces are drying, make and paint the signboard. Use the mat knife or single-edge razor blade (and work on a large piece of scrap cardboard) to cut the large piece of foamcore down into two smaller pieces, each 16″ × 26″. Cut the corners off each piece, following the diagram below.

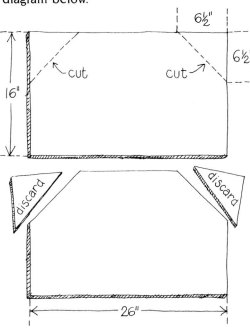

Glue the two pieces together with Sobo; while the glue dries, weight the pieces with heavy books to keep them from warping.

Mix a small jar of blue paint (bright blue plus a little white) for the background. Keep the paint fairly thick, with a consistency like heavy cream; do not dilute it with too much water. Paint the front of the foamcore sign and the edges (including the foam) with a smooth coat of blue. Let the paint dry and then apply a coat to the back, too. Repeat once or twice more, until the coverage is opaque. Let the paint dry completely.

5. Apply the glitter.

If you look at the photograph above carefully, you will see that glitter is applied on the front of the signboard to form a border 2"-3" wide around the sides and top but not along the bottom.

Brush some acrylic gloss medium on a small section of the left side of the signboard; sprinkle glitter on the medium while it is still wet. Blow away the excess glitter. Repeat this process, working your way around the side and top edges of the signboard.

When the glitter-sprinkled medium is dry, brush a coat of medium over the entire signboard to give it a shiny finish.

6. Glue the dough pieces to the signboard.

Arrange the dough pieces on the signboard, referring to the photograph on page 155 for guidance. On each red house place a door and three mosaic tiles for windows. It may take you some time to get everything properly centered and straight. When you have the pieces arranged to your satisfaction, lift each piece, apply glue to the back and replace it in position. Don't forget to glue the windows and doors to the houses. Let the glue dry thoroughly.

Framed Christmas Pictures

Each picture is composed of ½"-square mosaic tiles.

Photograph, page 156, for design and color guidance

1. Make the mosaic tiles.

Depending on how many pictures you want to make or which picture you choose to reproduce, divide the dough up and color each portion with paste food colors. Different pictures will require different amounts of dough. For example, if you are making the snowfolks picture (on the wall in the photograph on page 156), leave two thirds of the dough white; color a small portion of the remaining dough red, another little bit green, another bit blue and the last bit orange. For the Noel picture (on the table in the photograph on page 156), color half the dough red and half bright green. Take a small portion of the bright green and color it darker green. Keep each ball of dough tightly wrapped in plastic.

To make tiles, roll out the dough to ⅛" thick. Using a ruler and triangle for measuring, lightly mark the surface of the dough in ½" squares with the tip of a sharp knife. Cut the squares apart with the knife and carefully transfer them to waxed paper to dry. As the squares dry, move them around on the waxed paper so they don't stick to it; turn the squares over once or twice so they dry evenly.

2. Prepare the frame.

While the tiles are drying, prepare the frame. First release the spring clips from the back of the frame and remove the backing piece, the cardboard mat and the glass. You will not need the glass for this project, so dispose of it safely. Cut the cardboard mat into pieces as shown.

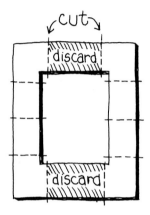

Work with the backing piece (which also has the hanging loops and/or easel stand attached to it) and the wallpaper or other pretty paper: Place the backing piece on a sheet of newspaper, blank side up. Spray it generously with adhesive. Quickly, while the spray adhesive is still tacky, center the pretty paper on it and smooth the paper down firmly on the backing piece. Turn

MATERIALS

Bread/glue dough (page 22)

Paste food colors (red, green, blue, orange)

Ruler, triangle

Inexpensive ready-made frame, 8½" high and 10½" wide
NOTE: The complete frame should include flat molding, glass, cardboard mat, cardboard backing piece and four spring clips holding the parts together.

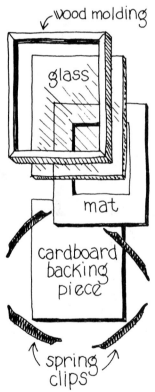

Wallpaper, gift wrap or other pretty paper, one piece 9" × 11"

Spray adhesive (the kind meant specifically for artwork and craft projects)

Mat knife or single-edge razor blade

Sobo glue

it over on a clean piece of cardboard and use the mat knife or single-edge razor blade to cut away the excess paper.

spray adhesive

Smooth

cut excess away

back

E

easel

Put the wood frame face down on a table. Place the paper-covered backing piece into the frame, paper side down. Take the pieces of cut-up cardboard mat

and fit one corner and one rectangle into each corner of the backing piece (lifting the easel stand out of the way if necessary). Replace the spring clips in position in each of the corners. The pretty paper will be locked firmly into the frame when the clips are correctly placed.

Turn the frame right side up.

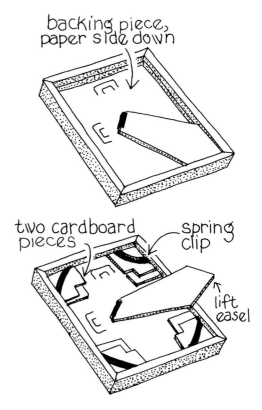

backing piece, paper side down

two cardboard pieces

spring clip

lift easel

3. Arrange and glue the tiles in place.

Using the photograph on page 156 for guidance or inventing your own design, lay out the tiles on the pretty paper (and on the wood frame, if you like). When you have the tiles arranged to your satisfaction, lift each one, put a dab of glue on the paper and replace the tile in position. Let the glue dry.

Paddleboard Wall Decoration

Photograph, page 160, for design and color guidance

1. Make the basic braided diamond.

Using wax crayon, draw a diamond 8″ wide and 10″ high on a cookie sheet or on the back of a jelly roll pan. Using light pencil, draw an identical diamond, centered, on the paddleboard. These outlines will help you shape the braided diamond before baking and position it correctly on the paddleboard after baking.

Roll three ropes of dough, each about 18″ long and ¾″ in diameter. Braid them snugly, starting in the middle and working out to each end, taking care not to stretch the ropes as you work. Transfer the braid to the cookie sheet or the back of the jelly roll pan and arrange the braid just inside the crayon outline to make half of the diamond. Cut off the ends cleanly at top and bottom.

Repeat to make the other half of the diamond, joining the two braids with water at the top and bottom.

2. Add the border of berries inside and outside the diamond.

Roll balls about ½″ in diameter. Attach the balls to the diamond by brushing water both between each ball and the diamond *and* between balls. Work all around the outer edge (except for about 2″ on each side) and all around the inner edge; check the photograph on page 160 for guidance.

3. Add the holly and berry trim to the diamond.

Mold six holly leaves by hand, making each one about ¼″ thick, ¾″-1″ wide and 1¼″-1¾″ long. Use the back of a knife blade to incise a center line in each leaf. Roll six berries, each about ¼″ in diameter. Arrange the holly leaves at the top and bottom of the braided diamond as shown in the photograph on page 160; then lift each leaf, apply water to the back and

MATERIALS

1 recipe of flour/salt dough (page 16)

Wood paddleboard, 9″ × 17″

Wax crayon; light pencil

Acrylic paints (brown, white, green, red); brushes

Polyurethane, brush, turpentine

Green crystal sugar

Five-minute epoxy

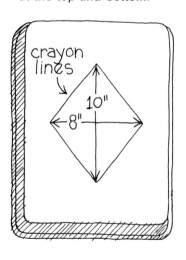

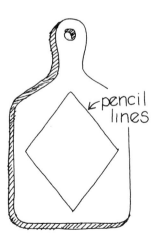

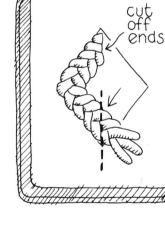

replace in position. Dot water on the berries and press them gently in place on the leaves.

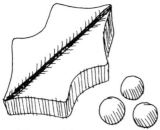

4. Make additional holly leaves and berries.

You will need six more holly leaves and nine more berries to trim the paddleboard; make them now, according to the instructions in step 3, and place them on the cookie sheet or the back of the jelly roll pan with the braided diamond. I recommend making one or two extra leaves and several extra berries, in case of cracking or other mishap.

5. Bake the diamond and the additional leaves and berries.

Bake at 250° for 45 minutes and then run a spatula under the diamond to loosen it. At this point the additional leaves and berries will probably be done, so remove them from the oven. If they are not done, continue baking but watch them carefully and remove immediately when they are done. Continue baking the braided diamond until it is completely hard. Remove it from the oven, let it cool and check it again to be sure it is indeed completely hard. If it is not, return the diamond to the oven to bake for a while longer.

6. Paint and polyurethane the braided diamond, leaves and berries.

Mix brown paint and water together to make a thin, light brown wash and paint *only* the braided diamond. Carefully paint one coat of white on the holly leaves and berries attached to the diamond. Paint one coat of white on the additional holly leaves and berries. Let the paint dry.

Now paint two coats of green on all the leaves and two coats of red on all the berries. Let each coat dry before applying the next.

When the paint is completely dry, brush two or three coats of polyurethane on the entire braided diamond and the additional leaves and berries. Let each coat dry thoroughly before applying the next.

7. Add the crystal sugar decoration to the braided diamond.

Brush polyurethane *only* on the top of the braided diamond. Sprinkle green crystal sugar on the wet polyurethane. Blow away any excess sugar. Let the polyurethane dry completely. When it is dry, the sugar will be firmly attached to the diamond. Brush another coat of polyurethane over the sugar to seal it. Let the polyurethane dry.

8. Glue the braided diamond and the additional holly leaves and berries to the paddleboard.

Center the braided diamond on the paddleboard, referring to the photograph on page 160 for placement. Note where the diamond touches the board. Mix epoxy glue; lift the diamond, apply glue to the board at the points of contact and replace the diamond in position. Arrange the additional holly leaves on the paddleboard, checking the photograph again for placement. Lift each leaf, apply epoxy to the back of the leaf and replace in position. Let the glue dry.

When the glue is dry, mix up more epoxy and glue the additional berries on the paddleboard and holly leaves.

Decorated Cookies

Photograph, page 160, for design and color guidance

MATERIALS

1 or more recipes of cookie dough (page 27) or any good sugar cookie dough

Christmas cookie cutters

1 or more recipes of decorator icing (page 29)

Paste food colors (red, green, blue, yellow)

Decorating bags

Icing tips
NOTE: I used #2 tips for almost all the decorations.

Small, soft brush for painting

There are two techniques used for decorating the cookies—painting and piping. Read all about piping on pages 29–31; painting is explained in step 2.

1. Make and bake the cookies.

Cut out and bake a batch (or two or three) of cookies from my cookie dough or your own favorite sugar cookie recipe. I used the following cookie cutters: bell; stocking; star with scalloped edge; two different cottages; holly leaf; candy cane; snowman; large scalloped round and small scalloped round to make each wreath; plain round plus diamond-shaped aspic cutter to make each Christmas tree ball. You should use whatever cutters you have or can borrow.

2. Decorate the cookies with piping and/or painting.

Read about piping on pages 29–31 and practice a little on waxed paper if you have never done piping before. Don't be afraid to try it—it's like drawing very simply with a crayon or pencil, and you certainly don't have to be an artist to do it or enjoy it.

To make paint for decorating, put a tablespoon of white icing in a little bowl, add 1½ teaspoons of water and some paste food color and mix briskly to get a consistency slightly thicker than heavy cream. Use a small, soft brush for painting; let the paint flow off the brush to fill in any area that you would like to be solid-colored. The paint is rather sticky and may take an hour to dry.

The instructions and drawings below tell you how to make three of the decorations that I made; you may want to adapt my designs to your cookie shapes or invent some designs of your own. If you like, change the colors to suit your own taste. Use the photograph on page 160 to give you ideas and inspiration.

Work in an assembly-line fashion on each group of identical cookies. For example, do step 1 on every bell and then step 2 on every bell and so on until all the steps are completed on all the bells. This is an efficient method and also gives the icing on each cookie time to dry a little between steps.

Bell: You will need blue, green and red icing, each in a decorating bag with a #2 icing tip, plus a little blue paint and green paint.

Star: You will need yellow, green, red, white and blue icing, each in a decorating bag with #2 tip, plus a little paint of each color. You will also need some small, round candies or slices of gumdrop for the centers.

Cottage: You will need all five colors of icing, each in a decorating bag with #2 icing tip.

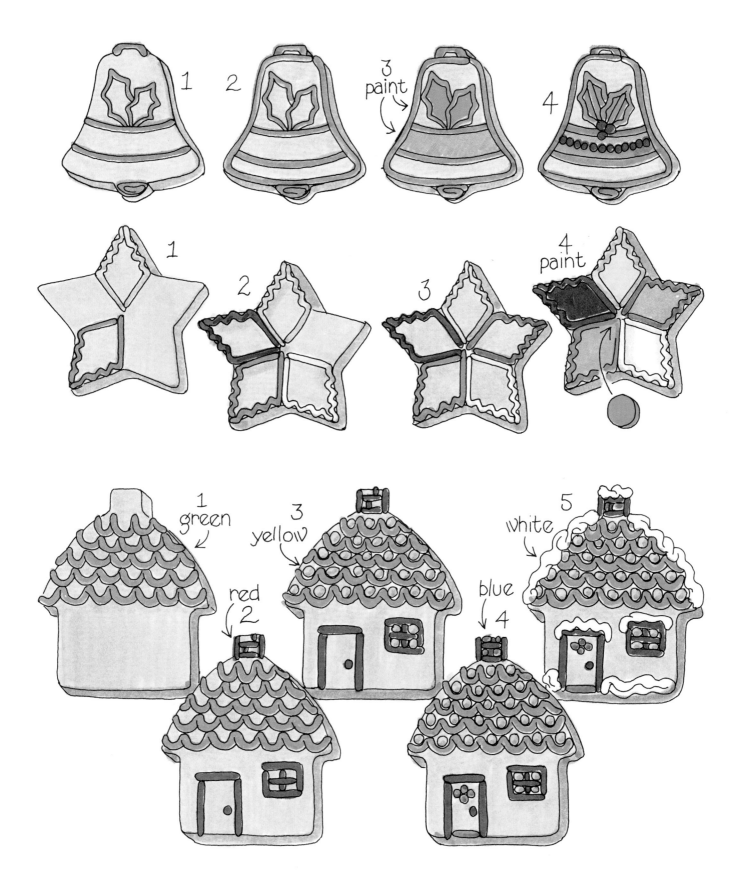

Index

OTHER BOOKS FROM SEDGEWOOD® PRESS: